BEACONS OF LIGHT

Inspiring people and places

BEACONS OF LIGHT
Inspiring people and places

Annette Barker

Copyright © 2025 Annette Barker

ISBN paperback 978-1-0685716-8-8
ISBN ebook 978-1-9192046-0-4

All rights reserved. No part of this book may be reproduced or used in any manner without written permission of the copyright owner except for the use of quotations in a book review.

Typesetting and cover: www.Shakspeare Editorial.org

DEDICATION

This is dedicated to those who have been and are my Beacons of Light.

And to those whose lives have not been blessed by such beings.

CONTENTS

Dedication	v
Preface	ix
A Sewing Box For Christmas	1
Claude	5
Jan	15
How Chicken Pox Changed My Life	19
My Beacons of Light: *Mes Phares*	22
Chiropractic: Philosophy, Science and Art	39
Mabs	44
The Cypress	50
Graylingwell, 1897-2001: History and Compassion	58
Digging Up the Garden: A Journal	77
A Nice Little Stranger	83
Words – Home And Work	99
Chichester Walls: Seasons	113

'Such Stuff As Dreams Are Made On'
A novella

Flight	121
Florence	128
Lathkill Dale	133
Bibliography	145
Acknowledgements	147

PREFACE

How this book came to life - a reason to live

When I finished *Our French Connection*, my small book of memories from my French childhood and youth, I ended on words suggesting that it might not be the final book, and that there was more to say. On this, I have been working for the past two years.

I pay tribute to my friend Carl who, as early as June 2023, wrote, 'I also look forward to watching again your process of reflection and rediscovery as you embark on book number two.' In spite of recent threats to the completion of this project, I have carried on; since he has not doubted me, why should I have doubted myself?

To go back to recent threats: in November 2024, I fell coming out of the shower at home. I have had a few falls in my life, and always managed to pick myself up and go on.

Not this time, though. I sat on the floor a long time trying to get my legs to work. I had a pain in my side (I later found I had cracked three ribs) and my head was hurting.

Eventually, I did manage to drag myself back to bed.

During the next few days, of which I remember chiefly the voices of children and grandchildren, I am told I was under end-of-life care. This happened twice within a fortnight, but I am here now, hoping to live long enough – and beyond – to finish this book and make it a companion to the first one, published two years ago.

My first small, slim book was primarily written for the grandchildren, to leave them memories of my early years in France. It was proofread by Jeff, who also assisted me with its publishing. Jeff was a man of many talents with whom I began to correspond, got to know well, promptly came to consider as a friend … and lost: all in the space of some six months. An undiagnosed cancer took him in a few weeks, shortly after he celebrated his seventieth birthday in the summer of 2023.

Now it is my turn to be hit by a bolt from the blue as, since those days in last November, I am more limited in what I can do with my body.

Limited because strength has not yet fully returned to my legs, and I still need a support to walk. Yet, this is improving and, after a long time in bed, after not sitting up for so long, after not putting a foot on the floor for three months, I have regained mobility beyond expectations. I have started on my daily walks again. What might I be able to achieve by the time this book is published?

With these thoughts in mind, I embarked on the revision of this book, which has been a renewed source of interest and enjoyment. I trust these pages are a tribute to all those who have been and remain for me *Beacons of Light*.

April–May 2025

Beacons of Light

A SEWING BOX FOR CHRISTMAS

Every year, Henriette looked forward to the Christmas show at her grandmother's theatre. No, her grandmother wasn't an actress. She was a cloakroom attendant in one of the oldest theatres in Paris. But the wonderful thing was that the son of a leading actor and the granddaughter of a cloakroom attendant were treated just the same: the same seats; the same bag of sweets and fruit for the interval; the same presents.

The first part of the show was pure magic. There was the auditorium, all red velvet and gold. The waiting. The hush when the curtain rose to reveal the huge Christmas tree on the stage. Just for that day, the actors turned into clowns and magicians. From time to time, they might call a child to come up on the stage. Henriette still shivered with excitement remembering last year, when she had been asked to hold some cards for a conjuring trick.

During the interval, she would go for a stroll in the foyer with her grandmother. She loved the feel of the polished floor under her feet and the sparkle of the chandeliers reflected in the mirrors. Then the bell would ring. Time to go back to their seats. Time for the distribution of the presents. Slowly, the curtain rose and there, under the tree, were mountains of gifts wrapped in multi-coloured shimmering paper.

Every child was called in turn to go up on the stage and receive a gift from a member of the Company. The only thing Henriette didn't like so much was that you always knew what you would get: a doll or a car if you were six; books if you were ten. The best ever was two years ago. She was seven and had got a portable writing desk. The top opened and the front flap dropped to reveal sheets of paper and envelopes in soft colours, pens, nibs – and a blotting-pad which you rocked right and left to dry the ink on the paper. She'd written letters to her family, to her friends, to all her dolls. She'd even written letters to herself.

But this year, she would be nine. Nine, for girls, meant a sewing box. Her heart sank. The only thing she hated when she went to the holiday club run by the nuns was the hour reserved for sewing every afternoon. Her best friend Nicole would turn out crisp white hankies, but Henriette's only piece of work had become all limp and taken on a funny colour – grey, with streaks of blood. And her thread always got into knots.

What was she going to do with a sewing box? She could have given it to Nicole, but her parents said it was ungrateful to give away the presents you received. They'd also said Henriette wasn't to go on about not wanting a sewing box. Grandmother was upset because her best friend, who had always collected the names and ages of the children for the presents, had died in October and someone else was making the list.

Henriette had sat next to Jean-Pierre last year. He'd been nine. He'd got roller skates. Nice. She'd asked if she could have a pair for her birthday, but her mother had said no. She thought she'd fall and hurt herself. Henriette knew she wouldn't because Nicole let her borrow her skates sometimes. But Henriette didn't tell her mother – it would only worry her. Maybe she'd get better at sewing when she got a bit older.

She enjoyed the first part of the show and the stroll in the foyer. She'd been good and not bothered grandmother about the sewing box.

After the interval, the distribution began. Henriette was glad her surname began with R because she had to wait a long time. And it was nice to wait a long time for a present. Even if it was a sewing box.

'Martin, Jacques … Morand, Colette … Pirard, Jean-Michel.'

Her stomach tightened. Her name would be soon.

'Raoul, Chantal … Renaud,' she stood up 'Henri.' She sat down again. 'Renaud, Henri, grandson of Madame Renaud, cloakroom attendant?'

Henriette looked at her grandmother. There she was, near one of the safety exits, gesturing to go on.

Henriette got up. Her legs felt weak. She walked down the side and climbed the few steps to the stage. She advanced towards the beautiful actress – tall, fair hair, in a blue velvet dress … She looked up.

'You're not a boy!', said the beautiful lady.

Henriette couldn't think of an answer. She tried to smile back.

'I'm so sorry,' said the lady. 'Your name was taken down wrongly. Henri instead of Henriette. I'm afraid you've got the wrong present – roller-skates – we can change them, if …'

'Oh no! Thank you!' cried Henriette. She took the parcel the lady was holding out to her and hugged it tight. 'Oh no, thank you very much! It's just what I wanted!'

CLAUDE

Claude was my brother. He was half-way through his twelfth year when I was born in the winter cold of February 1940. France was in the early throes of the Second World War against Germany.

We lived on the eastern outskirts of Paris. My father had been called up, following Germany's invasion of Poland and the subsequent declaration of war by France and the United Kingdom. He was a joiner who worked for a small firm.

There were five of us left in the house: my grandmother, my mother and her half-sister, Claude and me. My grandmother, at seventy-one, was fit and healthy – she had to be, as she took care of the home and the family needs while my parents were out at work. My mother was an accountant with one of the main banks in Paris. Her half-sister, Louisette, was blind and stayed at home.

In June 1940 – when I was four months old – my mother took the decision to leave Paris with our family. She did so along with the many Parisians who were fleeing ahead of the attacks which, according to the news, the Germans were going to unleash on the capital. An uneasy armistice had been signed on 22 June, following the entry of German troops into Paris on 14 June. It divided the country into two zones: the North Zone (*grosso modo* north of the Loire river) was occupied by the German forces; the area south of the Loire, where the government, headed by Marshall Pétain, had migrated to Bordeaux (and later to Vichy) was called the Free Zone and benefitted from less stringent living conditions.

Why, though, would the Germans bomb Paris, where many of their notorious leaders were enjoying a much easier life than the inhabitants? A difficult question to answer, especially with the wisdom of hindsight. But there were rumours that Hitler, before seeing Paris, had wanted to annihilate it; this was enough to instil fear in the population, whose reaction was to flee towards the Free Zone. Moreover, as far as my mother was concerned, the bank where she worked, then the BNCI, was transferring its main seat to the south, to Pau, a town in the Pyrénées. So, being the sole bread winner in my father's absence, she had no choice but to uproot herself as well.[1]

This movement of a whole population in chaotic circumstances became known as *l'Exode* (the exodus).

Imagine my mother in Paris, at the Gare d'Austerlitz towards the end of June. There were too many people for the space on the remaining trains leaving for the south. I have, thanks to the little she told me, been able to picture my mother successfully boarding one along with my grandmother, Louisette who was blind, my brother on crutches, and me, the baby. They hoped to find powdered milk for me at the various stops. They hoped to reach the south, not knowing whether

---

[1] "In 1940, with the invasion of France and then the Occupation, BNCI had to move the securities it held in Dinan to the free zone in Pau. It was done on 20 June, after a nerve-wracking evacuation that took five days." (BNP Paribas, 'Well of History' histoire.bnpparibas/en/bnp-paribas-at-the-heart-of-the-second-world-war/).

approaching planes at various stages during the journey were friends or foes.

We stayed near Meillon, a village a few kilometres from Pau, where my mother's bank had moved. We depended on the kindness of strangers, employees of the BNCI whose hospitality made space for us as best as they could. Claude went to the local school, another uprooting for him. My mother walked the few kilometres to Pau most days, sometimes being taken in a car if rationed petrol permitted.

What about our family home while we were away? My godmother had been obliged to stay in Paris because of her job; depending on the erratic train timetable, she managed to pay a few visits to our home and assure us that it was unharmed. The German forces occupying Paris and its neighbourhood were finding life there pleasant enough, and it soon became clear that Hitler's decision to raze Paris to the ground had been abandoned. The immediate danger of blanket bombings passed; businesses and people gradually came back to the North Zone. For us ordinary inhabitants, as long as we kept quiet and endured our share of rationing, hunger, cold and the general discomfort of an occupied population, we were left alone to get by as well as we could.

I am not certain when we returned home, but I know that life became even more difficult after 1942, when the whole of France was occupied by German and Italian troops. We did survive, though, and I have some early memories which prove that we were back in our house before the end of the war, and that my father joined us there after being demobbed.

Why do I not know more about those difficult years? I found my parents and my grandmothers reticent to talk in detail about them. It may be also that, when young, we are unaware of the importance of our elders' memories, and I did not ask often enough.

However, this is not about me, nor about the family at large. These memories are important when they concern Claude and how the war impacted his whole life.

Claude had been going to school until an accident meant he needed an operation on one of his hips. This took place shortly before the war broke out and seems to have been botched, leaving him with a limp for the rest of his life.

I never fully knew Claude. He was, as I grew up, more like an uncle than a brother. When I was very young, he was still recovering from his surgery, and I was under strict instructions to leave him alone. I remember sneaking into the downstairs room where his bed was, climbing on to the piano and pinching some of his calcium tablets – pinkish-brown and tasting of chocolate – which were the closest available thing to sweets at the time.

Eventually, Claude recovered, except for his limp, and had the same irregular access to school as his contemporaries. I recall he sometimes came home with a vitamin biscuit for me, having kept one from those dished out at school. I also remember that he had a passion for modern history – and by that I mean especially conflicts between France and Germany (or Prussia, earlier on); a passion for all things military; a passion for collecting any shrapnel he could find following some aerial conflict or some rare bombing raid on our neighbourhood.

Why, when the war ended, why was Claude not allowed – or better, encouraged – to pursue his studies? Why, as family lore would have it, did my father say to him, 'now, you've got to work'? Is this why I remember him mainly as bitter? The Claude I knew was a curious mix: timid at times; sudden rages erupting as a 'last straw broke the camel's back'. In turn taciturn or voluble. At times quiet, at others loudly irascible.

Was the chief reason for this rancour due to missing a career which would have fulfilled his love of the armed forces? Surely, that was the career he would have chosen. It would have been impossible for him to take up an active military position because of his limp. But there must have been office posts for which he could have trained, so that at least he would have worked in a milieu congenial to him.

Instead, he was apprenticed to a jeweller, a small firm specialising in the mounts holding precious stones in rings. Why? The reason I was given was that 'he was artistic, he was good at drawing'. Did this justify placing him with an artisan who was bound to suffer, first, from the dearth of spare riches which followed the war for most 'ordinary' people, and then from the inevitable mechanisation of small artisanal productions? This mechanisation happened, eventually, with the loss of jobs. My mother then thought of finding employment in her bank for Claude.

You could call my mother's banking career a happy chance, at least in one way. Having planned to become a teacher, she was, after her father died suddenly, taken on and trained by the bank in which he had worked. She was sixteen then, and loved her unplanned profession from the start. It could not make up for the tragedy of losing a close relative so young, but it did give her a chance she might otherwise have missed (having been a teacher all my life, I do not think she would have much enjoyed teaching).

She worked at one of the main banks in Paris, the BNCI, *Banque Nationale pour le Commerce et l'Industrie* (now morphed into *BNP Paribas*). It was reverently known in the family as ***La Banque***, the definite article excluding all others. It was therefore natural that my mother thought of this as the next step for Claude. Years later, she would have been happy to see me follow in her footsteps too, but I was resolutely impervious to the delights of accounting and wanted to become a teacher.

It was natural and beneficial, or so my mother hoped, for Claude to enter ***La Banque***. Alas Claude showed even less of an inclination and disposition than I for the calculation of compound interest. I remember him, sitting at the table after our evening meal, trying to study in order to pass some necessary exams for entering the banking profession, driven to tears by exasperation at some convoluted calculation. He did eventually pass these exams, but was neither happy nor very successful in his job – at least, not in his own view.

My parents seemed to conduct their own finances separately. This I know through some fragments I heard only later: the fact that my mother, feeling that Claude had been hard done by because he started work too young, never asked him for a contribution to the general expenses; my father's surprise, after my mother died, at discovering that there was much less in her account than he thought.

As far as I could make out, my father saw to the provision of food, much of it bought from the excellent market which stood outside our house on Wednesday and Saturday mornings. My mother dealt with other accounts, and loved spending any 'spare' on gifts and holidays. Claude, of course, had to broach the matter of contribution with my father after my mother's death, but I am still unsure as to how much my father knew about the arrangement with my mother while she was alive – or even after.

It is not my parents' fault that I know so little about this. They both loved me, sometimes with a love which I found a little too demanding. Hence, I craved more freedom and, from the age of seventeen, I lived away from home most of the time. As most adolescents, I had my own preoccupations, which I shared more willingly with my contemporaries than with my family. Moreover, it would have seemed presumptuous and improper to ask other members of the family about 'their' money.

Claude's chief pastimes were his books and his trips to Paris, or to the nearest town if he came on holiday with us, a rare occurrence. His bedroom was empty of all decoration – blank walls, clean surfaces, books lined up perfectly – and could have been a monk's cell. He usually spent Sunday mornings dusting and 'tidying up' his room – not that there was anything awry in it. He used the remaining time before lunch to look at one of his treasured tomes. My mother used to say that he turned the pages with great care, as if he might have found a large banknote hidden between them. Immediately after lunch, he took a train to Paris, where he walked in his favourite districts; his limp did not stop him until much later in life. He sat at the terrace of various bars, drinking coffee and watching the world go by. I remember my father asking him once, 'Why don't you go and breathe fresh air in the near-by fields?' To which Claude replied, 'I only breathe well in Paris!' He occasionally went to see a film – almost sure to be about war; or to an exhibition – likely to have an economic, political or geographical theme.

He was a loner. Whether he was always so, I have no means of being certain, since I did not truly know him when he was younger; but this passion for solitude and walking alone is among my earliest recollections of him.

He did have a girlfriend, Françoise. But alas, in spite of her very French name, her father had German origins, which were enough to cause in my father a measure of antipathy towards her (he did say to me years later, 'It's just as well your fiancé is English, I wouldn't have accepted him if he had been German', to which I replied that I was no longer a minor and would have done as I liked). His antipathy caused problems between Claude and Françoise; and a number of quarrels between my father and Claude ensued, with my mother attempting to step between the two to broker an unstable peace.

Not having heard about Françoise for many years, I thought the relationship between her and Claude had broken down. I was happily surprised to learn, shortly before his death, that they were still in touch and that she visited him.

At times, it was obvious that Claude felt unvalued, diminished, possibly unloved. This often arose from a comparison he held in his mind between him and me. He had not been able to pursue more studies after the war, whereas I spent several years training to be a teacher; his rancour on this point came in part from his being oblivious to the battle I'd fought against my mother's conviction that banking would have made me richer – it might have done, but at what cost! Another comparison was that we both became fond of someone with foreign origins, but he was discouraged in his relationship with Françoise, whereas I was not in mine with Chris. Were these differences imputable to the different times Claude and I grew up, times separated by the chasm of the Second World War?

It would be dishonest on my part to deny that I often appeared to be my parents' favourite, and yet I genuinely believe that I had done nothing to be so. Perhaps being 'a war baby', with the risks this implied, made me more precious in my parents' eyes?

Feeling that I could not be held responsible for this apparent preference, I wrote Claude a letter after I moved away from home. I assured him that I had not curried favours and was deeply sorry for these, aware that they were hurtful to him. I never had a reply, which saddened me. But I have to remember a greater hurt he must have felt. He told me that, after our father's death, he was coming out of our house when a passer-by asked him what he was doing coming out of there. 'I live here,' answered Claude. 'I am Monsieur Rouaud's son.' 'Oh, I knew he had a daughter,' came the reply. 'I did not know he had a son.'

I have to take Claude's word for this story, but I do not think he could have invented it. So, it erases all the unfairness I may have perceived in his attitude to me.

For years, I have tried to piece together Claude's attitude and reactions to me: his refusal to have me stay in the house when our father was ill in hospital, saying he did not want me to meddle with his stuff; irate telephone calls, which might be followed by pleasant ones; his looking forward to my visits towards the end of his life – according to the staff in his retirement home – when I went there, armed with his favourite cakes and wine.

Claude died a few years ago. It is too late to know what the truth was. I suspect it is a mixture of different truths, dependent on the latest conversation or event. Truths coloured in turn by unfounded or justified bitterness, but probably always by genuine pain.

Pain is pain for the sufferer. It hurts, whether justified or not in the eyes of the beholder.

JAN

I have just changed and stepped into the swimming pool. Ten past three. Twenty minutes before my lesson. Good – I'll have time to warm up.

I wave to Jan, who is standing waist-high in the water. She smiles and waves back, then turns towards a little girl wearing a fuchsia-pink swimsuit. Four years old, perhaps? Head on one side, wet, black ponytail falling on her right shoulder, she listens to Jan. She climbs out of the water. Jan stays in the pool and holds out her arms: 'Come on, I'll catch you!' The pink swimsuit leaps, the ponytail follows.

I swim a few lengths. Now at the shallow end, the girl is lying on her tummy, holding on to a float – a yellow starfish. Jan faces her, slowly walking backwards. Her arms loosely stretched in front of her, palms upwards, she lifts and lowers each hand in turn, showing her pupil how to kick her feet up and down. That lithe, lovely, little thing must be at one end of the age range Jan teaches. I am at the other – and I'm still having trouble with that trick!

Holding Jan's hand, the little girl is safely returned to her mother. Jan dries her legs and slips on grey slacks. She drops the float into a wire container, digs a few props out and walks to the deep end. She is slender, not very tall; her fair hair is short, her face slightly tanned; she is quick to smile, which brings out fine laughter lines at the corner of her blue eyes.

Looking at the props, I laugh.

'Heavens,' I say, 'circus tricks today!'

'Yes. You have to swim through a ring and fetch a brick from the bottom of the pool. How have you been getting on?'

'Not bad. Front crawl still not right, though.'

We start with that. Not brilliant – but maybe a little better. Then, the ring. Jan throws it in. It lands vertically on the bottom.

'You want me to swim through that?'

'Have a go!'

I try three times. No good. I come up, gurgling.

'Can't stay that deep!'

'Don't worry about it.' Jan laughs. 'Do you realise I spend my life teaching other people to float and you to sink?'

I can't help laughing, coughing at the same time.

'Have you swallowed a lot?'

'No, I'm fine.'

'Sure? Let's try the brick.'

She throws it in. It rests on the bottom of the pool, black upon turquoise. We did that last time, so I feel quite sure that I can. I swim towards it, dive – got it!

'Brilliant,' Jan says. 'How about the back somersault?'

'I'm still scared.'

'Shall I come into the water with you? Would that help?'

'Please!'

The grey slacks come off. Jan dives in. She treads water, curls up slightly, throws her head back … goes over … comes up again, the way she was facing. Perfect.

'Now, your turn,' she says.

Two aborted tries … some laughter … some more swallowing water. Let's have another go. Another try, I tread water. Suddenly I keel over backwards and come up facing the same way.

'That was great,' says Jan. 'Now, how about trying again to swim through that ring?'

So pleased by my recent success that I forget to be frightened by the depth, I pitch forward. I open my eyes. The ring is there … a little deeper … and I swim through it!

'That was excellent! We'll practise again next time.'

I have known Jan five months. After swimming badly for a lifetime, I was still terrified of putting my head under the water. I could not bear the thought of diving. As for opening my eyes under water – I just couldn't.

Then I decided it was time to try.

And I found Jan.

So, you could say I am succeeding. I still don't like the way I look in a swimsuit. I am not yet a good swimmer. Maybe I will never be.

But it's not just about that, is it?

It's not even just about swimming, is it?

It's about facing fear.

It's about trusting someone.
It's about living.

HOW CHICKEN POX CHANGED MY LIFE

When I was thirty-nine, I caught chicken pox. From my children? From the children I was teaching?

Wherever it came from, it hit me hard, and badly pockmarked my face for a while. At the time, our children being at the High School in Chichester during the day, I shared my spare hours between teaching at our village primary school and studying Italian for pleasure.

The year of the chicken pox was the year of my Italian A level. I had finished the written papers when the first spots appeared, and would be no longer infectious on the date of the oral, for which London University would send an examiner to the local College of Further Education.

No longer infectious ... but still pockmarked. I could not bear to present myself looking so, and asked London University for a deferral. This was granted, but I would have to travel to London.

And so it was, in the summer of 1979, that I stepped into the Entrance Hall of London University Senate House.

Oh, the shock of it all! Its vast space in a slender Art Deco. Its majestic proportions, the elegance of the staircase in front of me.

I recall being interviewed by a dark-skinned professor. I recall being asked why I was studying Italian at that time of my life. I recall trying to explain that it was, in some way, connected to my love of opera – and being asked, with a smile, what the point was, since one could never understand what they sang.

I recall struggling at times, but succeeding in the end.

Most of all, I recall being 'hooked'. London University had got me: I would make it my dream, my goal, my second home.

And so it was that I embarked on an Italian B.A., a five-year long, part-time course for External Students.

Education was so cheap in those days! A few hundred pounds bought me the inscription for the course, some books and some hours of tuition by correspondence from tutors associated with the Cambridge-based National Extension College (a virtual institution to me during my studies, but whose actual buildings I came across many years later, a short walk from our grandson's Hall of Residence).

Some of those tutors were good, others not so. One was exceptional, one of those people you never forget.

Of those five years, what remains?

A sense of elation and intensity.

I recall gradually honing essay-writing from wanting to say everything on a subject to seeking the few and relevant points necessary to answer a particular question.

I remember discovering the history of the language, deciphering some ancient text. I relive – and renew – the delight of finding an affinity with a particular author. All these akin to the slow amassing of a growing and multifaceted treasure.

And also: the meeting of minds over a particular text; some impassioned discussions sitting at a table and drinking tea in the refectory; the friendly arguments, the exchange, the sharing, the pleasure of a common pursuit.

Also precious, the quiet hours; the studious, solitary hours spent at a desk strewn with books in Middlesex South; the silence only interrupted by a brief hushed exchange with the librarians, the subdued gliding of the trolley bringing the requested books from the stack. Other times, high on the top floor, where I sat at one of the small desks set in front of every narrow window, ensconced between tall bookshelves rising to my right and left as my own bookends. And everywhere, the special scent of old books.

I recall all this – and I hear the sceptical, the rational, the all-knowing: 'Such delights cannot exist in a continuum; this is a fable; an illusion you are spinning.'

Believe or disbelieve as you will.

Those intensely lived times are what I choose to keep from those five years. None can be denied. Each was true then. Each lives on, true still. Each inhabits what remains of those years: my enduring love for all things Italian – language, culture, landscape.

MY BEACONS OF LIGHT: *MES PHARES*

In the course of my life, I have had the joy and privilege to know very special people, some known better than others, every one of them unique. Those people guided me for short spells or for ever. All have one point in common: every one of them introduced me to a richer, wider dimension of life. Many I think of as *balises*; others, rarer, are truly *mes phares* (lighthouses).

Mes balises

First, I want to thank my beacons, named *balises* in French. Their role is akin to that of floating buoys marking shipping channels in and out of port, or helping ships navigate as they pass over invisible sea routes. *Balises* do not have the strength, the majesty, the constancy of lighthouses. They mark our path for a while and then recede as we move on. But they all marked a turning point, a transition, a new direction which might never have happened, had they not been there.

Mes balises in France, in my younger years, were Éliane, Madame Roussez and Madame Gibelin. The former two reminded me that my true calling was NOT in banking but in teaching. The last introduced me to Camus. It seems I was privileged to be taught by such personalities in France. From my conversations with others, it appears that not everybody has had the good fortune to meet with such guides; with people who remain prominent in our memories long after we cease seeing them; people who inspired us, who showed us the way, who may have changed the course of our lives.

Éliane

Éliane was paramount in my love of English. Now that I have lived in England much longer than I lived in France, I see her influence as one of the most important in the long term, since it steered my life towards this side of the Channel.

But allow me a brief return to an even earlier time, to my first years learning English – and my beginnings were a disaster. In my first two years at secondary school, this subject was taught us, with little inspiration, by a teacher who had been told to switch to the new, fashionable method. This advocated the use of the foreign language throughout the whole lesson. Hence, the teacher had to stop using any French, she had to use English only, coupled with the international phonetics system. Having been trained in this myself as a young teacher, I can understand how difficult, how alien this might have been to someone who had taught for a long career by asking students to translate English into French, and vice-versa.

So, at the age of eleven, I could understand very little of what was said in class. With the unshakeable conviction of an eleven-year-old, I harboured the feeling that it was the teacher's fault. She looked to me of *un âge avancé*, though in truth she must have been much younger than I am now. Also, that she was *dépassée* (overwhelmed), struggling to teach according to a new method which had been imposed upon her. She certainly did not seem at ease, so I may not have been entirely mistaken in my assumptions.

It did not foster any early progress on my part, nor any liking. Indeed, I firmly resolved that, once I had passed the necessary exams, I would have nothing more to do with the language. How little I knew then of the fascination this rich source would inspire in me for a lifetime!

But come my third year, and a ray of light turned darkness into understanding. Our new teacher, Madame Bloch-Mason, was young, vibrant, beautiful (I remember her dark hair and her intensely blue eyes). She worked the miracle of replacing what was opaque by something clear, lit by interest and fun. After two years, she asked in the course of a conversation in English what we were hoping to do in life, and she did not laugh when I said I would like to teach English. Her reaction truly gave me confidence.

Later on, it was Éliane who helped inspire further my love of English and made me want to study hard for the sake of it, because it was a rewarding challenge. Even more importantly than giving me language skills, she saw that I was in the wrong place, on the wrong course, having followed my mother's wishes that I should study commerce and thus ensure a good career in 'The Bank' – that mythical entity which had been my mother's joy, had given her pride in her work, but which sounded to me like a hell on earth if I had to work there for a lifetime.

My Beacons of Light: *Mes Phares*

I can say that those two years, plodding along the dry path of commercial training, were only misguided in one way, since in another they meant I met Éliane, who taught me much, both in English and in values.

She was, I thought, a kind of Marcus Aurelius: strong, resolute, stoical. I did not know much about her private life, for she only alluded to it briefly from time to time. I was not very close to her, but met her occasionally as time went on. Her main influence, when I was fifteen, was to advise me when I felt somewhat lost in the maze of taking the wrong course. She did not hesitate to voice that I was mistaken to have chosen so, and thus was one of the great influences that helped me find my way back to a lifelong love: teaching.

Realising that I was on the wrong course was one thing, moving from it was another altogether. There seemed to be no way of convincing my mother to let me follow a university degree course. Her obsession, often and clearly spoken, was that if she died before I had finished these studies, my father's salary would be insufficient to support me and allow me to complete them.

With hindsight, it strikes me as sad that I had already been living in this country for several years when she died. On the other hand, since she was only sixty-four then, she may have been partly justified in her fear of 'dying young'. In truth, I think such thoughts never left her and, with them, this obsession that she did not want me to pursue a course I might not be able to finish. Too melodramatic? Possibly. But could she have helped her rather pessimistic view of life, which had begun, I think, well before my arrival, only to be made worse by the war years?

And so, while many arguments and counter-arguments went back and forth, and in spite of my unfulfilled wish to enter the Paris University, I was fortunate. Fortunate that I was given the opportunity, through studying subjects for which I had no interest, to meet someone who taught one I liked, English. Doubly lucky in being able to change my disastrous course thanks to having been, throughout school, a little younger than my classmates because I had been taught to read at home. So, when I started primary school at the age of six, as is the law in France, I was 'expressed' into the second year. This meant that I was, officially, one year ahead in my schooling. Hence, when I had finished my purgatorial two years of commercial training (and obtained the diplomas I would now be unable either to find or to honour), I was still young enough to attempt the *Concours d'Entrée à l'École Normale* which, in those days, benefitted from a certain prestige. It was a *concours*, not just an exam, which meant passing was not enough: you had to be in a proportion of top candidates to gain entry. This proportion was decided by the school itself, according to prestige and location.

So, having reached the highest age at which a student could attempt it, it was truly a case of then or never. I prudently opted for the *École Normale* at Melun, which took the first half of the successful candidates, rather than for the Paris school, which only took the first third. The school I chose was sixty kilometres southeast of the capital, but my reckoning was that it gave me a better chance of being accepted – and I was.

They were the three happiest years of all my schooling. Part of this happiness was that I had to be a boarder, which, in my eyes, began to free me from life at home and allowed me to make new friends through a wider circle of girls, whilst providing me with a measure of extra comfort and food, since I had the opportunity to come home most weekends. It seemed to me the perfect balance: freedom with comfort when needed!

It was interesting to have become one of the oldest in class when I was admitted to the *École Normale*, since I had often been the youngest. It did not worry me; if anything, it made me more thankful for having been able to read before I entered primary school. That fact sent ripples well into my teenage years – how far those early landmarks follow one.

Madame Roussez

In the year of preparation for the *Concours*, my French teacher was Madame Roussez. Her persistence, her repeated attempts to mollify my mother and convince her to let me go to the University of Paris at the Sorbonne for a four-year degree in English were of no avail. But what she did succeed in doing was to give me a thorough grounding in French literature, in essay writing, in the famous *Commentaire de texte*, which was one of the key points of the *Concours d'entrée* – a rigorous analysis of any text given, setting it into its period and outlining its stylistic characteristics. I loved doing this, for it combined my great admiration for French literature with an almost scientific examination of any text given us at random; a dissection of what made it special, successful, moving or amusing.

Madame Roussez was never generous in her marks. Essays were rated out of 20, and the maximum she would grudgingly grant was 14 – or possibly 15. If I dared smile because I had 'made it' and got the prestigious 15, she was prompt to quell my enthusiasm: 'Don't look so pleased, Mademoiselle Rouaud, remember that in the kingdom of the blind, the one-eyed man is king!' In spite of this acerbic humour, she was a great support and keen for me to succeed, either in a degree or, after her efforts failed to convince my mother, in my studies to become a teacher.

She never lost touch with me, insisted on my visiting her whenever I was in France, or requested that I made myself available, if at all possible, for the few days she might come to our area for a short holiday. Was she, perhaps, somewhat ... demanding ... difficult ... dogmatic? Possibly all three. But loyal, I think. She never called me anything other than *'ma petite Annette'*, even when I was in my fifties. She never lost interest in my work or family for most of our association. It saddens me that, towards the end of her life, she turned rather distant, especially when I failed to respond immediately to one of her letters. She was such a letter writer, a kind of modern Madame de Sévigné, who expected prompt returns from her correspondents. So, not a tender, gentle character, but one of the great influences on my life.

Madame Gibelin

As to Madame Gibelin. Ah, Madame Gibelin! She was our French literature tutor at the *École Normale*: small, slender, vivacious, sprightly, with such dark, sparkling, smiling eyes. As far as I remember, she did not always give us back our essays on time. But how she shared the treasures of literature she discovered. In my first year, she rushed in and announced triumphantly, Miss Brodie-like, 'Close your books. Just listen. I'm going to read you excerpts from Camus' newly published book, *La Chute*.' That was in 1957 and I had not read much by Camus. The pages Madame Gibelin shared with us were such a revelation, such a wonder! I then got absorbed in his larger and earlier novel, *La Peste*, then in his philosophical books, *L'Homme révolté* and *Le Mythe de Sisyphe*. I still have the notebooks of the quotations I copied. What discoveries they were! I remember those months as an intoxicating time, when there was so much to find out.

Three years later, in my last year, one of our group came into the room and announced, 'Camus is dead. He's been killed in a car accident.' He was forty-six. It was as if a light had gone out. Such a wonderful writer, such a wonderful man, such a loss to us all.

Those were my *balises*, my *points de repère* in France.

Mes phares

As steadfast beacons of light, they have had, and still have, such importance in lighting my way, in guiding and inspiring me. As tall lighthouses they stand, strong, steady, holding fast in any storm, casting their light far over the waves. For ships to take bearings, to feel hope revived as they find their way out of the unknown, out of the storm. Their light remains faithful, trustworthy, generous and reassuring.

Chris

To begin with, my reason for moving to the UK was Chris.

In the summer of 1960, I was due to spend a fortnight in London with Éliane to hone my skills in English, having just been nominated to my very first post: teaching English in a French secondary school to the younger, eleven- to fourteen-year-old students.

But alas, Éliane fell ill, and I had to make alternative plans. Thanks to my mother's contacts at The Bank I found hope. Her young colleague, Nicole, had spent some months as an au-pair with an English family in Shoreham-by-Sea.

'Shoreham-by-Sea!' I exclaimed, 'but that's not London!'

Indeed it was not, but London was easily reachable by train for the day, and I would have plenty of time to go there, since I was staying with the Watkinses as a paying guest. Isn't it ironic that, when I was hesitating, it was my mother who convinced me to accept this offer? I suspect she regretted this many times as this eventually led me to leave France and live in England.

For it was in Shoreham that Chris and I met, his mother being a good friend of my hostess, Mrs Watkins. Was it just chance? Or was there, after all, a reason for my not going to London with Éliane that summer? These questions cannot be answered, or rather, the answer depends on whether you believe in destiny or not.

We were very young when we met in the summer of 1960, and very young still when we got married three years later.

The 1960s now seem to me akin to prehistory or, as one of our daughters-in-law would say, 'mediæval'. The social mores were so different from the present ones, especially regarding young people living together before (or without) getting married.

Hence, we married before I left France. Our wedding day was a happy occasion, a day to celebrate, a day to see many members of my family before moving to England. The Channel was not a chasm and I thought that, as years went by, it would become easier to cross. I was right: when the UK joined the Common Market, travelling became easier and restrictions on imported goods lifted. Alas, I was also wrong: I had no reason, then, to think the disastrous 'Brexit' would happen. No reason to imagine such a severing of links. One of its negative consequences is that it now takes longer to check passports. It is not so bad for me, as I play the system with either passport, French or English, depending on which country I'm leaving or entering. But I still have to wait until my British husband's passport is checked. As far as the changes of mind by politicians allow us to predict anything, it may get even worse.

However, none of these shenanigans were known to us on our wedding day, and we trusted in everyone's ability to travel unimpeded, ours and our relatives'. We went away for a few days to Vézelay, a small town with a beautiful basilica, nestling in the Burgundian hills. After one last evening with my parents, we travelled back to England.

What was it like to arrive in a country which I had visited only on holiday? To enter a flat in Wilmslow which

I had never seen (although it had been the object of much correspondence – how often we wrote letters in those days). What was it like to live in this flat with very little furniture and few amenities?

The honest answer is, 'happy in some ways, difficult in others'. The flat we rented was in a large house, divided into apartments without much care for aesthetics. Chris was on a student grant doing research at the Jodrell Bank radio telescope. He often worked at night. We had no telephone, so if I wanted to have a few words with him when he was on duty, I walked down the road to the nearest telephone box.

I missed the job I had left in France, with its many students and colleagues whose absence I felt more acutely than I had imagined possible. A job would certainly have made it all more balanced but my diplomas were not recognised here. Those diplomas for which I had worked so hard in France, in which I had taken such pride! Thus hurt pride was added to the distress of lonely evenings and not being able to find work through traditional channels.

How those times now seem like the dark ages! I now know many young people who live together long before they marry or form a stable partnership. Whatever their official status, they usually find out together what they want to do and share, which jobs to go for, where they want to live. So often, if they get married, they have most of what they use in everyday life. They have no need of what my future sister-in-law called, causing me great puzzlement, 'a bottom drawer'.

I remember when she first asked me, 'Do you have a bottom drawer?' I had no idea what she meant. Did not all chests of drawers or cabinets have a bottom drawer? Our daughter's generation does not seem to know the expression, that it referred to objects you saved for little by little, scraping money from gifts, and putting them away until you were married: a milk-jug here, half-a-dozen teaspoons there. Presumably, you stored these in some bottom drawer, waiting for life together – and better furniture.

I am glad that the young people I know have more choice. That they are able to live together before deciding whether to make a solid partnership of it; able to find a job, a house to rent. The sensible thing would have been, surely, for me to come and live here, alone or with Chris, and see how the future shaped. But I know that would not have been possible when I was young, not without opprobrium and shock from parents and most other relatives. I still remember my mother, when one of my cousins became pregnant before her marriage, saying to me, 'Thank heavens you did not do that to me!' Did that *to her*? What a strange comment. I still hold the view that, overall, things are much better now. Whether it gives young people more stability, I do not know; some tell me it doesn't. But it is so much less hypocritical.

Despite beginnings so different from those of the present youth, Chris and I have 'lasted'. Our children gave us a large family party to mark our sixtieth wedding anniversary. It is, I hope, a witness to our love, affection, trust and determination that we are still together, many years after those first months in an old flat, now demolished and replaced by modern housing.

After what seemed a long stretch in Wilmslow, I still had no results from many job applications. Later, I found out that this waiting only lasted a matter of weeks, but it felt much longer when lived one day at a time.

At last, I found a part-time job, teaching French in a primary school. This meant having a new purpose and getting out of the flat several days a week. Chris went on to teach physics at Wilmslow Grammar School, and we started looking for a house to buy.

Over the years, jobs and houses changed. We moved from Cheshire to the South Coast, children came and grew up, and many grandchildren arrived, who celebrated our diamond wedding with us. I am thankful that we have travelled this far together. Chris has supported me through illness and through the many aspects of life together. Such a long association as ours creates solid bonds, and such bonds are precious at difficult times.

Other people have been beacons of light in my adopted country.

Mabs

Mabs was my gateway to so much beauty: to some children books I'd missed, not being brought up in England; to the beauty of English, to some of its texts, to Shakespeare, to other poets. She brought me so much beyond these, in the loyal friendship she always gave me.

She was, indeed, my best and longest-known friend and I shall come back to her.

Bill

A more recent friend was Bill, whom I met in the early 1990s. He knew me at one of my lowest times and it was he who helped me through a long stretch of depression. He was steadfast, supportive and did not abandon me when the therapy came to its 'official' end. I realise now, seeing in what dire straits the NHS is, that my acquaintance with him – both in the speed of referral and the length of treatment – was pure luxury by today's standards.

I do not believe that 'online' therapy can be as effective as meeting in person. Even though patient and therapist always observe distance in the therapy room, being in the same space as another human being, catching a smile, a look, the warmth of the voice, all these are special, and not so easily conveyed via a meeting on screen. This I know through personal experience, having been in person at lively meetings of examiners or OU staff, and doing the same by way of the internet. Communications online can be extremely useful, but they cannot replace human contact in some cases. A nurse, a surgeon, a chiropractor – to name but a few – cannot fulfil their vocation and help their patients solely via the internet.

Ralph

One person who helped me via 'distance-learning' – though it was by post then, not the internet – was Ralph. When I was in my late thirties and enrolled with London University, he became my Italian tutor. We did meet, but his primary role was to help me via the posting and marking of essays. He did much to introduce me to the treasures of Italian literature. He was the most conscientious of all the tutors I had over those years and spent much time writing comments and advice, in contrast to the tutor who contented himself with ticking any page he had scanned. Although his own problems made Ralph unavailable at times, he left me, from the many months I studied with his help, a legacy for life in my knowledge and love of Italian; and for this I owe him much gratitude.

Jeff

Late among those who have inspired me came Jeff. He was in my life for such a brief time, some six months. Six months during which he helped me edit, review and publish my very first, small book, in which I jotted down memories of my early life in France to pass on to grandchildren and further generations. Six months during which we exchanged so many emails. Six months during which we got to know each other and then, like a comet that lights up the heavens by its brilliance and disappears, Jeff went. Struck by an undetected cancer that took him away in the space of a few weeks. No warning, no signs. He had so many plans. Such a short association, yet it had depth, for I shared so much with him through the help he gave me with my book.

I shall ever be grateful to him, thankful for knowing such a man, thankful for his help in assisting me to leave some token of inheritance to my family. Thankful to his wife Jenny, too, for sparing him for so many of the moments he spent helping me. May the Lord in whom they both believe reward them in ways which I cannot imagine.

Without him, and Mabs, and Carl, the little book I published for my family and friends would not exist. Not in its present form, under its title of *Our French Connection*. Nor would it be in national libraries. It may not be widely read and consulted, but for me, who so love books and libraries, the thought of a little of me surviving in the reserves of these establishments is strangely comforting.

Mabs I knew for so many years, Jeff for so few months.

Carl

As to my young friend Carl, he has given me an introduction to a wider world, one that goes beyond the purely logical and visible. By introducing me to the philosophy that underpins chiropractic science, he has strengthened my resilience.[2]

His being both my chiropractor and my friend is a precious combination. He has helped me to be convinced anew that the heart and the soul can undoubtedly remain young, even as the body wears out. This has touched and comforted me deeply, and his support, whether at close quarters or at a distance, brings light into my life, even when age tempts me into despondency.

He wrote to me once when I was at a low ebb, 'Your light is not extinguished.' I believe him and, most recently, when many in the medical profession were predicting my imminent demise, he kept faith that I would recover.

I have, so far. I make the most of this chance; for it is a chance which, at one time, I had ceased to hope for.

---
2 See Chapter 'Chiropractic'.

These light-bringers, *mes phares*, and all the treasures they have brought and still bring me, are an integral part of my life. Without them, I would not be who I am.

Those who are the most important may well recur in various pieces and under other guises. Bill, a trusted guide at a dark time. Jeff, whom I knew for such a short time – the shortest association I have had with one of my light-bearers. Mabs, who was much my elder, and whom I knew for some sixty years (in one way the opposite to Jeff by length of association), the best, warmest, most generous friend one could wish for. Carl, one of the latest in date, much younger than I – the youngest, but so wise.

The length of a relationship is not a measure of its importance in our lives. Nor is age. It is the light such people bring that makes them special, for they are as bright stars who illumine our skies.

Such have been and are those who bring light, courage, inspiration. Some have passed on, some are still here. To all I owe an immense debt of gratitude. They influenced, coloured, enriched and go on enriching my life in such a way that all are now integrated and intertwined in the person I have become.

CHIROPRACTIC

Philosophy, Science and Art

Depending on your internet search or on your interlocutor, you will come across different definitions of chiropractic, and different opinions as to its efficacy.

It is sometimes defined as a hands-on treatment of the spine, or as a holistic therapy because it cares for the whole individual; it is often classified as one of various complementary therapies.

Views on chiropractic are as varied as its definitions. For some, regular visits to their chiropractor mean the maintaining of their good health. For others, chiropractic is a complementary medicine to be used only in crises. And there are those who express disbelief as to its benefits.

Let us go back to the source of chiropractic. At the beginning of the twentieth century, its founders, D.D. Palmer and his son B.J. Palmer stated the importance of the spine in the preservation of good health. Their insistence on a natural way of preserving health rather than treating established disease provoked, at times, the ire of the medical profession; it even led to the trials and imprisonment of some chiropractors.

Throughout trials and controversies, chiropractic has endured. The 'preservation of good health' remains the core of its philosophy and methods. This is present on the website of the Chichester Chiropractic Centre, which defines it as 'a method of spinal adjustments that aims to encourage alignment of the spine ... a harmony of science and philosophy with the aim of helping the body to function at its optimum.'

The preservation of good health also figures in a manual studied by chiropractors in training; this defines chiropractic as 'a philosophy, science and art of things natural, a system of adjusting the segments of the spinal column by hand only, for the correction of the cause of disease.'[3]

The above definitions point to the salutogenic nature of chiropractic, shifting the focus from what makes people ill to what makes them healthy. It does not deny the role of other practitioners, nor the indispensable help of emergency medicine in crises. This I know through personal experience. But I also know that I have benefitted over many months from the care my chiropractor has given me.

In non-critical circumstances, which we can call 'normal', chiropractic views the health of the individual as tightly connected to the spine, as it acts as a fast highway for the messages which govern the person's activities. If it does not function well as this 'highway', there is dis-ease in the way in which messages from the brain are relayed to the body – and vice-versa.

For the role of chiropractic in 'normal' circumstances, I go back to Dr Serio when he writes, 'Chiropractic has the word *chi* in it, meaning "life energy." Chiropractic also has the word *chiro* in it, meaning "of the hand." This

---

3 David Serio, 33, p.8, Bill Decken, quoting Stephenson's *Chiropractic Text Book*.

profession is literally a profession of touch designed to release life-force.'[4]

The two key words in Dr Serio's definition are *touch* and *life force*. The skilful chiropractor will use *touch* to sense the state of the spine and the patient's reactions. They will then *adjust* the spine to remove, as much as possible, the obstacles (called *subluxations*) that impede or slow down communication between body and brain. The aim is to increase the patient's ability to receive as much *life force* as possible.

Hence, the chiropractor is the mediator whose sensitive and skilled *touch* aims to improve communications within their patient.

We all know what touch is. But what is meant by *life force*? It is best defined by chiropractic's first principle:

> There is a universal intelligence in all matter, which continually gives to it all its properties, and actions, thus maintaining its existence.[5]

This *universal intelligence* is present in us as what chiropractic calls *innate intelligence*, a *life force* that is released by the adjustments applied to the spine.

One contributor to *33*, Dr Arno Burnier, was raised as a Catholic and suggests that '*universal intelligence* appears to be a safe term', unlike '*God*', which has led:

> to countless wars and unimaginable suffering.
> … Would anyone claim that his or her universal

---
4 Serio, *33*, p.79.
5 Serio, *33*, p.1.

> intelligence is better or greater or different than someone else's universal intelligence? ... Universal is universal after all.[6]

The paragraphs above present the three elements of chiropractic: *science,* in the chiropractor's knowledge of the human body; *art* in the chiropractor's skilful use of hands and knowledge; *philosophy* in the 33 principles which underpin chiropractic.

Are all chiropractors equally attuned to these principles? It seems not. Nor are all patients interested to the same extent in these same principles. But for me, the principles are one of the reasons why chiropractic works and hence, I see no separation between the adjustments made by a chiropractor and their consciousness of these principles. This combination is what produces excellence, and excellence demands time, patience and dedication. Such virtues can greatly enhance the life of patients.

Why do I have such faith in chiropractic?

One of the main reasons is that it does not abandon anyone. It believes that everyone, whatever their age and condition, can be helped by having their spine regularly checked. It also believes in the astonishing power of the body to heal, to recover. Surely, we can all verify this by the way our skin will scar and heal, or our bones mend.

I take comfort and strength from my conviction in this healing power, having survived various challenges

---
[6] Serio, *33*, Arno Burnier, p.2.

to my health, despite: a number of health professionals predicting my impending demise; being on end-of-life care twice; and being under palliative care.

My own chiropractor is modest. He always insists on his role as a go-between, who facilitates the link from *universal intelligence* to my own *innate intelligence*. His role is to remove obstacles that prevent my ability to heal by 'measuring nerve interference, choosing the art of when or how to reduce or remove this interference, and then stepping back and allowing life to happen.'[7] Thanks to his help and care over the past years, I have witnessed my own improvements and ongoing recovery. This, and my continuing interest in the philosophy underpinning chiropractic, have strengthened my belief in its power.

I am convinced that chiropractic is, indeed, a science, an art and a philosophy. And I share the belief that – as you will often hear it said by those who find it helpful – it has 'added life to my years and years to my life'.

---

[7] Serio, *33*, Pam Jarboe p. 81.

MABS

When I arrived in this country over sixty years ago, I knew few people. But I was soon to meet Mabs.

Mabs was the head teacher of the very first school where I taught, Chorlton Park Junior School near Manchester. She was my introduction to an English junior school, and she so excelled in her job that no one, in the few schools I have known either through our children or through my teaching, has been able to match her.

I had just arrived in England and found it difficult not to have a job, after three years happily teaching English in France. Fortunately, this did not last long, and I know that Mabs and Chorlton Park were a part of my salvation.

Having applied to various schools without success, I then directed my letters to the Local Education Authority – and Manchester's Education Committee was remarkably good (we noticed the difference when we moved away after eight years). Finally, I received the offer of an interview at their offices in Deansgate, where I met with a Mr Powell. I hope he reaped in heaven the benefits of his kindness and generosity on the day of the interview for, a week or so later, a letter came – penned in the most elegant italic script – offering me a part-time job of several hours a week, teaching French for a pilot scheme called 'French in the Primary School'.

And so it was that Mabs and I first met in October 1963. The fact that she had appointed me as a pioneer to teach French in her Junior School was characteristic of Mabs. She was always keen, as the enlightened head teacher she was, to give the children who attended her school as many opportunities as possible.

In France, I had been teaching English to secondary school students, now I was to teach French to English juniors – it promised to be an interesting reverse experience!

I remember the school as bright and welcoming. The classrooms were arranged on either side of a central corridor, and the walls along that stretch were either used for displays on various topics, or lined with shelves for library books. There was also a tropical fish tank, which added to the liveliness. This was another tribute to Mabs' imagination, making maximum use of a narrow space to transform an ordinary corridor into an environment rich in colour and knowledge.

Mabs was supportive, and my colleagues, including the deputy head, were friendly and helpful. I enjoyed my new job, as pupils seemed to enjoy the new experience of learning French. The course included projecting images to illustrate the lessons, and there was even a serial filmed in France, called *La chasse au trésor*. Such teaching aids may be commonplace nowadays and some even vainly pretend to replace the teacher. In those days, though, they were novel and exciting, and meant as an adjunct to carefully planned lessons.

The children had fun doing a little acting during some of the lessons. We built a model of a French village (with my husband's help). I wrote a simple nativity play in French, which the children acted; and to end the year, they performed a longer play which I adapted from a French fairy tale. But I particularly remember our first piece of acting, a short scene about shopping. Mabs took a number of photographs, and I still recall that the shopkeeper was Ian and the client Sally – it is odd to think they will both be in their late sixties or early seventies!

However, not all children enjoyed French. In particular, I remember Peter from the top class, aged about eleven. I was walking around one day, looking at the children's work and stopped by him. He was making musical notations.

'Peter, you are not doing your French?'

'Non, Madame Barker, I'm composing.'

He was right to enjoy music, for you may well have seen or heard the famous concert pianist Peter Donohoe. I don't expect him to remember much about French at Chorlton Park, but I especially remember the way he played almost nonchalantly on the piano in the hall while we were waiting for Miss Cockayne – Mabs – to take assembly. The piece I remember most is the *Emperor Concerto*. Every time I hear it I am taken back to those far-off mornings.

From being colleagues, Mabs and I became friends. In time, this friendship included my family. She introduced me to many treasures of literature. She shared with Chris and me her favourite places in Cheshire and further afield. When Chris was working, she took me to National Trust properties, and so I became fond of Bess of Hardwick and her niece Arabella Stewart. I enjoyed visits to Haddon Hall and became acquainted with the beautiful black and white Little Moreton Hall. Eyam also has special memories, since Mabs introduced me to the way the villagers behaved in an epidemic of plague, isolating and sacrificing themselves for the good of others.

Our children were born, Mabs was godmother to two of them and took the third one under her wing when his own godmother died. A godmother in French is *Marraine* and she is as close a person as family, sometimes closer. So, amongst us, she became *Marraine*, and that is still how we talk about her. When the children were very young, *Marraine* lived in the next street to ours and, once they were big enough, they would cycle or walk to her house and play with the toys she kept.

After eight years, Chris got a job at Chichester College, and we moved from near Manchester to the south of England. But it takes more than distance to alter friendship. Friendship endures. Even though it was painful to leave Mabs, and yet another loved school, and colleagues I knew well, distance could not have killed such a strong bond. Mabs came to visit us. For some school holidays, she lent us her cottage in Over Haddon. It is still there, still called 1, Dale View – well named indeed, for from the bay window in the lounge, the whole of Lathkill Dale was on view.

I sometimes went to stay for a weekend while Chris kindly held the fort and looked after the children. Mabs and I had meals at the cottage or in one of the surrounding villages. We went to Bakewell on Saturday mornings, did some shopping, visited neighbouring villages at well-dressing time. Mabs took me to Stratford, and these visits were such a revelation.

Our children are now adults and have their own children, but *Marraine* has remained *Marraine*. When dear Mabs was unwell, she was perhaps a tenuous presence, but still so real and so full of all the memories we shared.

She is no longer with us, and yet she is. She copied for me John Clare's poem, 'Love lives beyond the Tomb'. It does indeed live on, for Mabs and all the riches she brought us.

I went to Over Haddon in October 2023, passed the beloved cottage which Janet had left to Mabs, and stepped into St Anne's churchyard to see Janet's beautiful memorial sundial; this brought Mabs close to my heart again, thankfully and painfully because I still miss her.

Janet was a special person for Mabs, a true sister-soul. They were both single, both had other friends and family, but their jobs brought them close to each other. They were able to spend all the time they wanted together and had so many plans. It was such a tragic loss for Mabs that Janet died so young and so unexpectedly. Cancer, not detected until too late.

After Janet died, Mabs' friends contributed to a memorial to celebrate and pay tribute to such a special being. We were honoured to be part of this. The result was a perfect sundial, made by David Kindersley – with some lines from George Herbert. On that October day, as the sun came at last out of the clouds after a drizzly day, I saw gnomon, hours and writing shine anew, cleansed by the shower. It brought tears to my eyes as I imagined us on one of our favourite walks, talking as we used to. We would both be 'old' and yet so young at heart. We could share so much with each other.

Yes, I still miss my very dear Mabs so much. But the tears were a witness to our long friendship of so many years.

THE CYPRESS

Laura fell in love with cypresses on the way from Pisa airport. They stood guard as the coach passed brown fields, and climbed up the hills in the distance. They made her feel instantly at ease, in this light so different from that of her English home. During her few weeks in Florence, punctuated with excursions around Tuscany and neighbouring regions, cypresses became her constant companions.

A few were growing in the garden which surrounded the hotel and, if she leant far enough, she could just see the tallest one from her window. Every morning, when she pushed the shutters open to let in the light, she would greet that tree softly, 'Good morning, beautiful!' What the sombre *cameriere* at the desk downstairs would say if he knew she spoke to trees, she could well imagine. There was a word for it in Tuscan: *grullo*, a bit soft in the head.

Soft in the head or not, she was lucky. She had started to learn Italian in her thirties and had secured a place on a course run by the University for Foreign Students. She found it all absorbing and thoroughly enjoyable: speaking Italian; listening to lectures on history, literature and art, also in Italian; and, on most Saturdays, a guided visit within the city or an excursion further afield.

Most of the students were of a 'normal' age and they came from all over the world; hence the enforced and welcome immersion in their only common language, Italian.

There were only two other mature women: Denise, a recently divorced Londoner who had decided to learn a foreign language as a kind of lifebuoy; and Nancy from Boston who, until three months ago, had spoken no Italian at all; she had come with her husband (somebody in Evangelical circles) who had been sent to Florence for three years. Most others were in their twenties. Françoise was on a long stay from Paris and Leif came from Stockholm; both were intent on making the most of their time on the course. Justin, the youngest and on a semester abroad from Texas, was not so keen on hard work and added an impish touch to the small group who often had lunch together at the *mensa*, the University canteen. The food was good if simple, the tickets cheap – a bargain, provided you didn't mind clearing and wiping the table yourself.

Since the course fees and lunches were so reasonably priced, Laura felt justified in allowing herself a few luxuries. Besides, on account of what she saw as her respectable age, she was conscious of the need for some privacy. So, she had chosen a hotel on the road climbing towards Piazzale Michelangelo, rather than digs listed by the University. Most evenings, she walked down into town for a late meal on her own, often in a trattoria she knew well by now. If she didn't fancy going back into the city centre she would stop at the small grocer's shop at the end of Via Romana and buy provisions for a snack in the hotel garden. Signora Santi was perfectly happy about such an arrangement as long as one bought a drink from the bar.

Laura would sit contentedly on an old stone bench, munching the barely salted bread, a few thin slices of cured ham or a chunk of parmesan. In the fading light of the warm June evening, she would pour herself a glass of the ruby-coloured local Chianti from the quarter bottle she had bought at the bar and drink it slowly, listening to the cicadas and watching the first fireflies begin their dance around the trunks of the cypress trees.

One afternoon, she was standing on the balcony of the University annexe, a little way north of the city boundaries, humming to herself, watching tiny lizards darting between crevices in the wall below. The distant hills were blue in the haze and the immense dome of the cathedral rose over the orange roofs of Florence, framed between two groups of cypresses. Laura heard footsteps behind her, turned around and smiled to Nancy, who closed the shutters of the French window carefully before joining her.

'That was a nice tune you were humming,' said Nancy. 'What is it?'

'I think it's out of an opera called *Mignon*, can't remember who wrote it. It's something like "Do you know the land where orange trees bloom?" Or maybe it's lemon trees. Not that there are many here.'

'It's a lovely tune.'

'Yes, I like it. It seems to fit in with the light here. With all the cypresses and olive groves.'

'Do you have many in England? Cypresses and olive trees, I mean?'

'Not real cypresses, no. It's too cold, too changeable. You can buy something a bit like them, but they're not the real thing. Not so straight, not so dark. They get messy as they grow. Olive trees …'

Justin bounced onto the terrace, leaving the French window wide open behind him. 'Hi! What are you two talking Italian for?'

'That's what we're here for, isn't it?' replied Nancy.

'Sure, but I find it hard as hell. Hey, have you seen the guy who teaches art history?'

'Bertoli? He should be here soon. But you'd better close the shutters, or we'll have another lecture on air conditioning instead of getting on with the Baroque.'

Nancy had reverted to her own language to talk to Justin and, whilst he dodged back into the lecture hall between the closing shutters, Laura thought how oddly the nasal American twang resonated in the Tuscan light, how it seemed to change Nancy's personality.

There were no lectures or visits on the following Saturday and Laura decided to go to the Certosa. *Professore* Bertoli had recommended an exhibition of manuscripts relating the life of Saint Benedict, on display for a while at the old monastery perched on a hill.

Laura took a bus from the station. On the outskirts of the city, the number of passengers – who had been tightly packed, jolted and shaken at every traffic light – thinned out a little, and Laura was able to stand by a window at the back.

As they climbed a steep hill, the bus slowed down. The houses became more spaced out, allowing views over fields, vineyards and olive groves. The bus came to a halt in front of a *vivaio*, a nursery. Rows of bright geraniums, young oleanders in terracotta urns, lemon trees in square wooden tubs and there, close to the road, a row of tiny cypresses, no higher than a few inches. So, cypresses also had to begin very small. Her friend in the hotel garden had not always been tall and aristocratic! Pretty stupid, really, not to have thought about that before, she told herself.

As she walked up the dusty path and several flights of stairs to the monastery, she turned back from time to time to soak in the colour and warmth of the surrounding hills. She could see ochre, white and red houses dotted around the terraced fields – and everywhere rose the blue-black fingers of cypresses.

'I wonder how long it takes for tiny ones to grow into one of those.'

Then she entered the monks' refectory and lost herself in contemplation of the richly gilded initials and the jewel-coloured, intricate borders.

A monk in a white robe took them round the cloisters, showed them a cell and explained the long-established pattern of monastery life.

In the gift shop, she chose some postcards and a bottle of bright-green liqueur. You could buy a small glass of it for tasting, and she sat on the terrace, relaxed by the warmth of the liquid, which tasted of aromatic plants and sunshine, looking at the softening haze of late afternoon spreading over the distant slopes. If she bought a tiny cypress, then she could take it back to England and plant it in a sheltered place. In a few years' time, she would have a corner of Italy in her garden.

During the time she had left, she embroidered on that theme every time she caught another glance of cypresses. On the way to Siena, she knew how she was going to wrap up the young tree and lay it tenderly in her suitcase. On the road to Mantua, she decided to buy a large terracotta urn when she returned home, and place the cypress in it. On the last, narrow, uphill stretch to Urbino, she pictured it standing on the stone patio in front of the house.

On her last day, she took the bus from the station again and got off at the *vivaio* on the way to the *Certosa*. The pit of her stomach felt empty, tight – as if she was about to meet someone loved and missed. She strolled in, admiring the lemons that were turning a pale yellow on their diminutive trees, softly humming her *Mignon* song.

The tiny cypresses were at the end, on the left, looking helpless. How tall were they? Ten, twelve inches perhaps? How long would one of them need to become four or six times her height?

The owner of the *vivaio* was advising a customer. 'No, I certainly wouldn't attempt to transplant a lemon tree into your garden here. In the south, yes, but here they have more of a chance in tubs. Do you have a conservatory? I would put it there in the winter. Otherwise it's not warm enough, you see.'

Not warm enough. Laura looked at a baby cypress. She saw it slowly dying in its terracotta urn, blown about by the sea winds, frozen by the unpredictable icy blasts of March, drenched by the capricious summer rains. And if it lived? If it grew taller than the sloping slate roof, taller than all the trees around it? How would it look in the middle of her English garden?

She remembered Nancy's American accent jarring in the warm Tuscan afternoon. There was such a thing as the right setting for the right object – or the right people. The Renaissance had a word for that: *decoro*.

'Anything I can do for you, Signora?'

She looked at the owner, smiled, felt herself blush. 'No, thank you, not for the moment. I was – I'm just looking.'

He turned to attend to someone else. While he was facing the other way, Laura slipped away, first pretending to be absorbed in the lemon trees, then gradually joining the path out of the *vivaio*.

She decided to walk back to town, hoping the long way down might calm her a little. She felt bruised inside. Bereft of her plans. 'For goodness' sake, it's only a tree!' she told herself. And yet, unreasonable as it was, it hurt. She stopped after a few steps. Looked back. Might it survive after all? Could she change her mind? It was now or never, her flight was early the following morning.

She turned and walked away from the *vivaio*, back towards the city.

That evening, she dressed carefully for her last walk into town. She would stop on the bridge and watch the swallows circling over the Arno. She would take one last loving look at Brunelleschi's dome, towering against the salmon-coloured evening sky. She would have her last supper in the trattoria in via San Lorenzo. She would not forget to slip a coin into the *Porcellino* fountain in the *Mercato Vecchio* and rub the nose of the small bronze wild boar, polished by the hands of so many tourists: it meant she would be back.

She leant out of her window, closing the shutters before she went out. Her tall friend was standing there, such a strong, upright cypress. She smiled and whispered, 'Good night, beautiful. I love you!'

When she landed at Heathrow, it had just rained and shreds of clouds were blowing across the sky. After being conveyed on moving pathways, after following signs along endless, blind corridors, she paused in a vast room where carousels were spinning, spewing out the luggage from incoming flights. As she waited, a notice attracted her eye: it warned against the dangers of introducing pests into Britain through the illegal import of plants. She smiled. 'Never mind about that – what about what Britain might do to some plants?'

She sighed. And said to the little cypress she had left in Florence, the little cypress that would grow strong and tall in the Tuscan sun, 'Farewell, beautiful. Be happy!'

GRAYLINGWELL, 1897-2001

History and Compassion

> On June fifth last year, a small part of the building was handed over for occupation, and on July 26th, although the workmen were still in possession of the building, the difficulty of finding room for patients was so great that G.C., a female patient, suffering from acute mania, was admitted, and the Asylum was thenceforth considered open for the reception of patients.[8]

Thus writes the Medical Superintendent of the West Sussex County Asylum, Chichester, in his *First Report* on the hospital. On 16 December 1897, a few months after the admission of G.C., the Asylum was reported in full occupation.

Until the end of December 1893, patients from the administrative counties of East and West Sussex and the county borough of Brighton had been cared for in the Sussex County Asylum in Haywards Heath. However, recorded minutes from the West Sussex County Asylum deplored the lack of places for new patients in other county asylums, such as Hampshire, Middlesex and Surrey. It was even advised, at one time, to send such persons

---

8 'First Report of the Medical Superintendent West Sussex County Asylum, May 27th, 1898', *W.S.C.A. Rules, Regulations, Annual Reports 1898-1899-1900*, p.16.

to a workhouse, or as far as Derby.⁹ It was evident that additional accommodation was required for the number of patients coming from such a large area, and West Sussex County Council set about planning for the care of those in need. Land had to be purchased, agreements and contracts to be drawn up.

As regards the land, one early evidence is a draft memorandum between *The Visiting Committee appointed by the County Council of West Sussex for providing an Asylum for pauper lunatics* and one William Smith, dated February 1893, which has a plan attached.¹⁰ This land had been part of a Royal Warren for breeding game in the early thirteenth century and had become farmland by the beginning of the sixteenth. The plan shows Graylingwell Farmhouse surrounded by numbered plots. The Church had a tenancy agreement with William Smith up to the early summer of 1895. Soon after, the Visiting Committee appointed by the County Council gave the Graylingwell Farm tenancy to John Heaver of Bosham, farmer (as witnessed by a detailed agreement drafted on 3 July 1895), *'for two years from Michaelmas 1895 at £247 a year'*.¹¹

Work began promptly. The building was staked out in May 1895, following the contract drafted on 18 January of the same year between the builders and the 'Visiting Committee appointed by the County Council for Providing a Separate Asylum for West Sussex'.¹²

---

9 *Ibid.*, pp. 27, 57–58.
10 'Draft Memorandum of agreement between William Smith, farmer of Chichester, and the Visiting Committee … for vacant possession of land', HCGR 6/4/3; Plan, copy 14756, 8 December 1892, showing farm in possession of William Smith, scale 6" to one mile.
11 'Report of the Visiting Committee July 1894–March 1898', West Sussex County Lunatic Asylum, *Minute Book 2*, p.48.
12 Ibid, p.27.

As regards the references to *asylum* and *lunatics* in various documents, we need to remember the original sense of those words: *asylum*, from the Greek meaning *inviolable*;[13] *lunatic* to refer to someone who was mentally ill, and not meant as an insult. Compassion towards those mentally afflicted and without sufficient means is evident in the original rules of the establishment. This compassion became clearer to me while I was searching through various documents. It seems to have inspired many aspects of the planning for this new asylum, as is shown both in the facilities for the residents and in the rules set out for the staff who were to look after them.

The compassionate attitude these papers reveal towards *pauper lunatics* is impressive and I could not help thinking, 'What about wealthy lunatics? What about poor Mrs Rochester, locked up in a third-storey room of her own mansion by her own husband, and hidden from all, not as a human being but almost as a wild beast – or worse, perhaps, as a mere object of shame?' However, since *Jane Eyre* was written half a century before the opening of Graylingwell, we may hope that by 1898 hiding lunatics as objects of shame no longer took place.

The Medical Superintendent's *First Report* describes the building thus: 'The Asylum is erected from designs by Sir Arthur Blomfield & Sons upon the modern Pavilion System, and is constructed of red Cranleigh brick with artificial Stone dressings.'

13 Also, Late Middle English (in the sense 'place of refuge' especially for criminals, via Latin from Greek *asulon* = refuge, from *asulos* = inviolable). It is interesting that in Italian *asilo* refers to a kindergarten, or to the right of asylum for a fugitive. It also referred to a psychiatric hospital, before these were officially abolished in Italy in 1978 by the Basaglia law. Basaglia was a psychiatrist who studied the care of patients for many years, and advocated shifting this care away from hospitals towards the community.

He obviously took pride in statistics:

> The Building covers 7¼ acres of ground. The actual roof area is 4 acres, having 2 miles of ridges and hips, over 21,000 sq. yds. of slates and requiring 120 tons of sheet lead. In the construction over 11 million bricks have been used, nearly 9,000 yards of pitch pine flooring, and 2,000 yards of wood block flooring. There are over 1,600 windows; 722 yards of corridors and 1,256 yards of subway. The soil drains aggregate to a total length of 2 miles, those for rain water 2½ miles, and together they require 314 manholes. There are 4½ miles of piping, 18,000 sq. ft. of gilded heating surface, 21 miles of wire for electric light work, and 15 miles for bells, telephones, etc.[14]

The most striking of the original buildings – and now one of some remaining – is the water tower, whose silhouette still dominates the skyline as you travel from the east towards Chichester. According to the *First Report*, it stands 90 feet above the ground, and various contracts suggest May–June 1896 as a likely completion date.

This tower does not stand exactly on the place of the well that gave its name to Graylingwell. The Asylum sank a new well a short distance east of the water-tower, to a depth of 80 feet, with an internal diameter of 7 feet. From the sump at the bottom of the well a 12-inch boring carried on to a total depth of 410 feet. There were two underground tunnels at the bottom of the well for storage, each about 82 feet long and 6 feet high. At the top of the water tower was

---
14 'First Report of the Medical Superintendent, May 27th, 1898', p.8 et seq.

a hard water tank of 23,000 gallons; below it was a soft water tank of the same size; and between the two tanks was water softening apparatus.[15]

There always was water on this spot. Before the well there were springs. But there were not, it seems, any graylings. Early records suggest a Saxon origin for the name, *Graegel's springs*. Under Henry II, we find *Grenyngeswell* and *Greningewell*; then, *Greilingewell* under Henry III, who granted it to Ralph II, Bishop of Chichester on 23 December 1243. The following year, Ralph II left it in his will to his Church of Chichester under the name of *Graylingenville*.

What about the provisions for the well-being of prospective patients?

Care for these patients as *people* is obvious in the *Regulations for the West Sussex County Asylum Chichester* published in 1890.[16] For instance, in a concern for recreational facilities in the *First Report*, based on the opinion that 'Recreation ranks with occupation as a most valuable agent in the treatment of the insane.'[17] It comes as no great surprise, therefore, to read that the Recreation Hall was a large room fitted with a stage and scenery, and that each ward was provided with games of chess, draughts and cards, as well as with books and newspapers. There

---
15 'First Report of the Medical Superintendent, May 27th, 1898', p.13. I am indebted to Katherine Slay, former librarian at the Chichester Record Office, for assisting me in finding these details.
16 'Regulations Pursuant to the 275th Section of the Lunacy Act, 1890' (Charles Knight, Printer, Chichester).
17 'First Report of the Medical Superintendent, May 27th, 1898', p.19.

was a piano in each block, a bagatelle table for the women, and a quarter-size billiard table for the men.[18] There were also outdoor activities in the form of walking expeditions and a football club.

This idea of recreation as a contribution to patients' well-being was developed in the *Second Report*, in the Superintendent's comments upon a performance given by Members of Staff as being:

> greeted with shouts of laughter and applause from beginning to end ... In the case of a mentally infirm [a good laugh] becomes a real medicine, of which a dose may so affect the stationary melancholic, as to prove the starting point on the road to recovery, or to rouse the apathetic and demented to a more active interest in their surroundings.'[19]

Some words in this report – *insane, mentally infirm, apathetic, demented* – may sound harsh, opposed as they seem to twenty-first century 'political correctness'. Yet, in the context of those years, they seem to me to be witness to a genuine human concern for those so afflicted in mind.

The staff had many responsibilities. The Superintendent's were onerous in terms of time and energy: 'He shall visit as many of the wards as possible, and see the patients therein, at least once in each day, affording to all patients frequent opportunities of communicating with him.'[20] How remarkable that the importance of communication for people in distress, who

---
18 *Ibid*.
19 'Second Report of the Medical Superintendent, May 26th 1899', p.14.
20 'General Rules For The Government Of The Asylum'.

may feel totally isolated, should be outlined so early!

Attendants and nurses had a long working day, even longer than nurses have today, from 6 a.m. to 8 p.m. The Rules of Conduct enjoined the Staff to be:

> patient, gentle, firm, and persevering in all efforts to induce the Patients to take food, to work, to join in recreation, and to perform in a proper manner the multiform duties of everyday life. ... bear in mind that [Graylingwell] is a Hospital, the sole object and aim of which is the recovery of those whose recovery is possible, and to improve and ameliorate, as far as can be effected, the condition of those whose disease is of an incurable nature.[21]

These are merely statements of intention, of course, and we all know instances in which reality bore little resemblance to documents that promised much. It is difficult to know how these Rules were translated into everyday life, and even more difficult to know how the patients who inaugurated the asylum perceived them. No doubt the new 'residents' varied in their reactions.

However, we do have the opinions of patients, families and staff, originally published in the 1950s in the patients' magazine, *The Wishing Well*. These are gathered, together with oral contributions, in 'Beneath The Water Tower' realised by The Graylingwell Heritage Project:[22]

---

21 *Ibid.*
22 'Beneath The Water Tower', The Graylingwell Heritage Project, 2015. www.graylingwellheritage.co.uk.

> Yes, Tuesday night was cinema night in the big hall.
> I think in earlier times they'd have variety shows and
> what have you, but when I was there they just had a
> cinema, Tuesday night. Males on one side, females on
> the other, nurses patrolling and never the twain shall
> meet. (Former patient, p.36)

> You worked as a team. The first thing was, the patient
> came first and it didn't matter what happened, the
> patient came first. Then you gave a first-class service to
> the staff. (Former member of staff, p.39)

> I think the image of mental hospitals at that time
> was that they were dark and awful places, and full
> of people who were miserable and so on ... But in
> actual fact there was a lot of innovation, there was
> a lot of experimentation, but there was also a lot of
> humanity and I think some of the people recovered
> from the effects of their illness by being in a wonderful
> environment – lots of space. They had reasonable
> food, they had reasonable interest in them without
> people being unnecessarily prying and they recovered
> simply because ... their biology and their psychology
> was given a chance to get back into some sort of kilter.
> (Former doctor, p.39)

Apart from such personal recollections, there was evidence of care and compassion in some of the Committee's decisions. For instance, that the words *pauper, lunatic* and *asylum* were to be absent from everything intended for the use of patients in the First Report; this is echoed in the gratitude of the Superintendent for the Committee's decision 'to allow the Institution to be called, for unofficial purposes, "Graylingwell Hospital", thus sparing the patients the dreaded stigma inseparably associated with the name Asylum.'[23]

The determination that *asylum* was not to be used, with a view to sparing the feelings of patients and their families, bears witness to the transformation this word had undergone: from its original meaning as a place of refuge, to that of a mental institution for those deemed too ill to be looked after by their own family or community. Personally, I regret the temporary loss of the true meaning of this word, which I find consoling and life-affirming against intolerance and self-righteousness. But since it had acquired shades of darkness, of fear, possibly of condemnation for those unfortunate enough to need it, we must acknowledge the spirit which inspired this 'loss', and pay tribute to the intelligence and compassion of that time.

Be that as it may, over many years Graylingwell cared for patients whose minds were unable to cope with the demands of life. Over many years, it tried to improve their mental health and, when there seemed to be little hope of improvement, to alleviate their distress. There were rare occasions when the buildings were put to another use, as when Graylingwell became a casualty hospital during the First World War.

---

23 'Second Annual Report of West Sussex County Asylum', p.18.

Then came a wind of change: 'Attitudes towards mental health had become more progressive from the 1930s as new treatments and changes in nursing styles moved the profession away from the former Victorian approaches.'[24]

I had occasion to be an out-patient at Graylingwell much later than this, from 1991 to 1993, years in which I saw my clinical psychologist about once a month. The access to him, and the length of the treatment, bore witness to the relative generosity of the NHS system at the time. Nothing like this could take place today; since then, huge changes have occurred – some with good outcomes, some with dire consequences.

My years of contact with Graylingwell were at a time when *Care in the Community* was hailed as the panacea which would achieve a double result: free the patients from bondage; and free the NHS from considerable expense. Was the intention genuine? We can give it the benefit of the doubt, since it aimed to give more freedom to people who may no longer have needed to be residents. Was the intention pure? No. One of its main goals – if not the dominant one – was to save money, since the old asylums were often in need of repair, modernisation or simply upkeep. Both goals are well summed up in this excerpt:

> Continuing advances in psychiatric treatment from the 1960s onwards meant that the need for psychiatric hospitals changed. … There were more community-based options for patients, and those in hospital tended to be in for a shorter period. All of these facts, together

---
24 'Beneath The Water Tower', p.46.

with the passing away of the older generations of long-stay patients, meant that the population of Graylingwell Hospital was down to 300, a figure which had been 1,150 in 1956.

Frances Russell, who took over as Chief Executive in 1993, reports that the Graylingwell estate was then costing over £1 million a year – money spent on the buildings alone – money which could have been far better spent in providing services and putting skilled staff in the community.'[25]

Indeed, the enthusiasm for reform and the better use of resources seemed to energise many in those years, which were also the years when, after leaving the *asylum* of my treatment, I endeavoured to use my own experience to provide advocacy for those in-patients who needed support during and after reviews; to contribute something to the local group of Mind; to do a little public speaking to explain the aims of *Care in the Community*. Like those around me, I believed in it for a while: it seemed to promise both more freedom and more choice for those leaving either the shelter of their ward, or the reassurance of their consultant or nurse.

I do not remember precisely the reasons why my share in these activities gradually died down: a certain disenchantment? The realisation that committee meetings were more talk than substance? The awareness that those for whom I had advocated would be left without a true refuge? My gradual distancing from these activities

---
[25] 'Beneath The Water Tower', p.52.

may also have been due to the limited readership of the magazine locally published by Mind; and to my realisation that I could dare move away from the safety of therapy and from much connected with it. It meant that I felt confident in moving forward to resume my more demanding, former roles in teaching.

In spite of my limitations in both time and energy, those years were interesting and worthwhile. Perhaps they gave me a little more insight than most of my acquaintances might have of such an environment during that period.

I go back to the enthusiasm for reform which, as well as much-needed money-saving, seemed genuinely to inspire the advocates of the new solution offered by *Care in the Community*. In the words of Frances Russell: 'money which could have been far better spent in providing services and putting skilled staff in the community.' Praiseworthy intentions, but what did they amount to in the end?

For more on this, I now hand over to someone who knows a lot more about this than I do, Barbara Taylor. Having herself been ill, and a patient of such a hospital as Graylingwell over many years, she combines both personal experience and thorough research in her book, *The Last Asylum – A Memoir of Madness in Our Time*.[26]

Barbara was a patient of Friern Asylum in the north London suburbs. She spent many periods of weeks and

---
26 Barbara Taylor (2014), *The Last Asylum: A Memoir Of Madness In Our Time* (Hamish Hamilton).

months there, seeing various psychiatrists, going through some gruelling experiences. In spite of all the difficulties, hers is a journey fascinating to follow: stark at times, informative, never self-pitying; a glimpse of life in this enclosed world and of some of the personalities she met there. I have no personal experience of being an in-patient, but I did benefit from a long association with my own clinical psychologist and, like her, found the official end of this therapy difficult to face.

Like her, I have one question: 'How would I fare if what happened to me back [then] happened to day?' She adds: 'Like the asylums in their heroic foundational phase, community care arrived on a tide of transformative optimism.' Her conclusion is bound to be ambiguous:

> So are things better now?.... Rapid change there
> has certainly been, especially at the organizational
> level, where one government-led restructuring after
> another has left everyone – managers, staff, patients –
> disoriented and anxious. Have these changes resulted in
> better patient care? The situation varies from service to
> service, place to place, so any broad-brush assessment is
> tricky. But a closer look at the language of mental health
> policy is revealing, taking us into a Humpty-Dumpty
> land of keywords – 'recovery', 'wellness', 'choice' –
> whose meanings, as in the case of Lewis Carroll's prolix
> egg, depend on the power of those employing them:
> a topsy-turvy world where it is easy to lose track of
> the distinction between sense and nonsense, crazy and
> sane.'[27]

---
[27] *Ibid.*, pp.250–51.

Friern has now become Princess Park Manor, a 'celebrity address, home to a bevy of pop singers, TV entertainers and football stars.'[28]

Back at Graylingwell, the last patient and the last staff left the buildings in 2001. The NHS occupied some of the buildings as offices until 2009. The site was sold to Linden Homes, which redeveloped it as Graylingwell Park, building residential houses in part of its grounds. It is fair to point out that these new dwellings have been planned so as to leave plenty of green space, trees and footpaths which residents and others are free to enjoy.

A 'social hub' has been created by transforming the former chapel into a space available to the public, inside which are display units on the development of Graylingwell. Indeed, this chapel is witness to the conservation orders that both Friern and Graylingwell enjoy, thus protecting some important buildings. From Barbara Taylor's account of the remains of Friern (whose former and present incarnations I do not know personally), it seems that more original buildings may be left in Graylingwell, where the chapel and farmhouse have been Grade II listed, and the park has been added to the register of Historic Parks and Gardens. The infirmary, mortuary, corridors, recreation hall, kitchens and workshop block have been demolished, but a number of other buildings erected in the 1890s are still standing: the main entrance, the clock tower and all the wards.

---

28 *Ibid.,* p.245.

What about the care of those patients who may still need the services Graylingwell and Friern once provided? This varies, as pointed out by Barbara Taylor, depending on which postcode they happen to live in. Regarding Graylingwell again, since it is better known to me, some provision has been made for the mental health care of some patients in new-build units.[29] In spite of this, reservations were expressed by one of the people on the Mind Committee:

> There were the long-stay people, and their view really was, 'What are you talking about, moving me on?' … The other people … on the whole they viewed it as probably a good idea … I think both lots of people, what they most worried about was losing the grounds and the feeling of asylum, somewhere safe.'[30]

This is echoed by a comment from my own former therapist:

> You can't have somebody that's been in a hospital for thirty-five years suddenly to be put back into the community. Well, I don't think you can, and he couldn't cope with that.[31]

Barbara Taylor goes back, in her concluding pages on various therapies, to some present methods of dispensing

---
29 'Beneath The Water Tower', p.52
30 *Ibid.*
31 *Ibid.*

care for troubled minds:

> CBT is the modern face of Anglo-American psychotherapy ... I do not doubt that – done intelligently and sympathetically by well-trained therapists – CBT can help some people feel better, at least for a time (studies of it longer term are inconclusive) ... This is not to be sniffed at.[32]

How do you define *longer term*? How many years? The CBT in which I took part some 30 years ago was under the guidance of such a sympathetic therapist as she mentions. To work out its longer-term effect, I would have to – or so it seems to me – take out of those 30 years all other factors which may also have helped me: this is not possible. My own conclusion, therefore, is that those CBT months gave me a great deal of help: some needed at a time when I was in distress and which may have become unnecessary; but also some strategies that have been useful since then in coping with everyday problems, and are still useful today. CBT seems to me an eminently practical kind of therapy; it may not rest on deep philosophical principles – or if it does, it does not quote them to the receiver. Yet, in the hands of an empathetic therapist, it can be a guide for many situations and problems that occur in daily life, whether at the time of therapy or later on.

For my part, I am convinced that there was in that therapy, its views and its methods, something which contributed to the way I now view life and cope with whatever it sends my way. Indeed (as I have thought

---
[32] Taylor, *The Last Asylum*, pp.260–62.

about it again, following the passing of my former therapist after a long illness), I am the same person as the one who benefitted from his care; the same yet different in that I have grown, as we all do. So, the person I am now is woven from multiple strands, among which those of CBT therapy are very strong. How could I fail to be thankful for its help, which allowed me to come out of a dark tunnel and look outwards more widely?

Where I agree with Barbara Taylor is when she expresses further doubts on some types of CBT now available:[33]

> The NHS now offers computerized CBT, so that a person suffering from anxiety or depression can be sorted out without any human interaction whatsoever – and this despite the fact that a host of studies has shown that it is the quality of the relationship with the therapist that determines the outcome of CBT, as it does with all therapeutic encounters …

Nor am I, for the same reasons, convinced about therapy by means of online consultations with a professional therapist rather than a machine. I feel the presence of two living beings in the same room is essential to healing. A tone of voice, a look, a gesture, warmth, compassion – all these are difficult to capture online.

I have to acknowledge that 'online therapy' may seem the norm to the generation of our grandchildren, who never knew a world in which online access did not exist. Nevertheless, it seems to me that, often, the proximity of a

---

[33] Taylor, *The Last Asylum*, p.260.

human presence is essential to heal another human being: 'Healing occurs in the presence of presence.'[34]

As to Graylingwell and similar places, as one who received care and compassion for a while as an out-patient, I am not oblivious to the hardships that may have been perceived in the former service, especially by those who felt they were locked up there by some uncaring agency, be it a doctor or their own family. Whatever a patient's perception may have been, it is unlikely that people were 'locked up' by their family in Graylingwell, for:

> there was a requirement for a report to be written on potential patients by both a doctor and a Justice of the Peace. This would have definitely reduced the chances for a family to get someone 'locked up'. Also, given the pressure on beds, it is unlikely that the hospital would wish to keep someone as a patient who was not perceived as insane.[35]

However, this does not mean that no patients escaped feeling imprisoned.

In conclusion, I acknowledge the time and help – the *asylum* – Graylingwell gave me for a while. History proves it gave many others who needed it the same *asylum,* right from the days of its creation. I am grateful for its care, and still wonder whether there is, for those seriously

---
34 Serio, 33, p.107.
35 Katherine Slay, former librarian at the Chichester Record Office.

distressed and devoid of financial means, any form of *asylum* available in our modern society – a society which likes to think of itself as super-efficient; a society which, in terms of human contact, can feel isolating to all of us, well and unwell.

DIGGING UP THE GARDEN

A Journal

Thursday 28th July

I've dreamt of a white garden since seeing Vita Sackville-West's at Sissinghurst. Today, we visited Barrington Court Gardens in Somerset. They are laid out in three 'rooms' designed by Gertrude Jekyll, and one of them is a white garden.

Saturday 30th July

Dreaming is fine for a start, but the only way to get things done is to get on with them. We've decided that a good spot for a white garden might be a patch at the bottom of our front garden, against the hedge. Chris, my husband, has cleared it before and has laid a path around it, but it has reverted to a semi-wilderness. I'll start clearing it tomorrow.

Sunday 31st July

I wake up with a sinking heart. What have I let myself in for? I'm no natural gardener. I can't dig that patch. It's hot and sticky, and I've no energy.

Still, I make a tentative start after breakfast. The main and recurrent invader is bindweed. Roots everywhere, deep, intertwined, mixed up with everything else. A mess. Inevitably, it conjures up the image of all I've yet to sort out in my life. Don't tell me it's a bit of a cliché, I know that. A platitude. But it doesn't stop it hurting.

I have to pause. My back is aching, and it's not easy to blow my nose or wipe tears with earth-stained gardening gloves on. Don't give in, though.

Monday 1st August

I go back to the digging and clearing after breakfast. After a bit, I have to stop, like yesterday. There are things I miss. People I miss. One of the things I miss is feeling confident in any long-term projects. I used to, years ago – or is it that the past always appears better, simpler than it was? No, I did, really. Perhaps depression, whatever it really is, tends to deprive us of this trust in the long term? Perhaps it takes so much energy to get from morning to evening that, when we emerge after months of just doing that, we've lost the ability to plan too far ahead? Do we ever recover this ability? After how long?

Well, I've climbed out of the worst pit. I've had a lot of help. I've worked hard; we've worked hard. The sense of structure hasn't come back yet, or at least not in any way that could be called 'permanent', but maybe that's not to say it won't ever. In the meantime, and that's one of the things I've learnt in the course of many months, I have to make one goal, one reachable goal. That's why I have got to persist in this.

When I stop today, I've cleared the central patch. Two faithful roses, which have valiantly bloomed in the wilderness for many years, now stand clear. 'Peace' and 'Papa Meilland'. Perhaps we can transplant them to another part of the garden.

I've also discovered with great joy that a clump of lily-of-the-valley has survived, brought many years ago by my father from our old house in France. It is one of my favourite flowers. The French give it in fragrant bunches to those they love every May 1st. One of my floras says, 'spreads when happy'. It hasn't spread much these last few years, that's hardly surprising. Next year maybe?

Tuesday 2nd August

Late morning start today. I carry on along the hedge. I turn up big clods of compacted earth mixed with flints and roots.

One thing that really gets me about me is this: I don't think there's too much wrong with my reasoning. When it comes to understanding, I feel as sane as the next person. But do my emotions follow? Oh no. No such luck. They lag behind, tug at my sleeve, look back – seldom in anger but often in sorrow. Why can't they just rally round, keep pace, behave?

I bash the new lump of earth so hard that it sends bits flying all over the place. Then the thought comes into my mind that, perhaps, emotions are a bit like children who are not being difficult, but just being children; who need persuading, coaxing, encouraging, rather than coercing and bullying; children who can only go at their own pace.

And if others are willing to allow me my own pace, why do I have to be harder on myself than they are?

I don't hit the next lump of earth quite so hard.

Thursday 4th August

I can see the end in sight. It has become more of a pleasure (because it is, after all, a manageable challenge?) as I have gone on.

I try to be careful, but there are many bulbs in the corner I'm digging up at the moment, and it is impossible to avoid the odd one getting speared by the fork. Here is another platitude (or perhaps it is a prime truth?): healing hurts. Or, as it was put to me once, 'no pain, no gain'.

Of course, it is a shame about the few bulbs that get hurt. But do I want to let the weeds take over further just to save these few? No. So, go on. There is no viable alternative.

Friday 5th August

I've done it. The patch is clear. Over the past few days, I have been thinking of all that could be planted in this white garden, a luminous and healing place. Certainly a lace-cap hydrangea. White lamium, one of them is a must, it is called 'Sissinghurst White'. A white rose. Maybe, for a touch of colour, a sea-holly tinged with blue?

'When can we start planting?' I ask Chris.

'Oh, I don't think we'd better put in any plants or shrubs before spring. Some of the weeds will come up again, and it gives us a chance to tackle them when they're small.'

I am reminded of the Little Prince, whose tiny planet was so infested with baobab seedlings that he had to remove them carefully every morning. Otherwise, they would have taken over and, eventually, destroyed the planet.

So, there's no telling, just now, what our silver garden will look like next year. True, the patch looks a lot better than it has done for a while.

What about my life? Does it look better than it did a while ago? Perhaps, I am not always the best judge of that. But I think it does. I hope so. Others, who matter, tell me so.

Chris sees the disappointed look on my face at the thought of leaving the plot fallow for the winter. He smiles. 'Of course, we can plant new bulbs for the spring. These will be fine.'

Of course, we can. I will choose every bulb so lovingly. Narcissi, especially. Some creamy, luscious double heads, some delicate ivory single blooms. No, they are not meant to take the place of the fully matured white garden in my mind. They are just a slow and realistic beginning. You can replace a cooker or a fridge just like that, but not something that has slowly taken shape in your mind, not someone you have grown to know and love.

I'm not looking for replacements. I'm looking for patience.

The bulbs will help with that, I know. And also, I hope, give pleasure to others and to me.

A NICE LITTLE STRANGER

'And what's the bill likely to be?' Hannah asked.

The voice of the mechanic at the other end of the phone reeled off various technical terms, tagging a price on to each of them, and concluded, 'So, you're talking about four hundred pounds, plus VAT.'

No, you're talking about it, Hannah felt like replying. But she merely said, 'We'll have to think. I'll give you a ring on Monday.'

She put the phone down. Why take it out on the mechanic, who had been quick in diagnosing the trouble and had even offered to put her back on wheels tomorrow? How was he to know that the little phrase 'you're talking about' infuriated her, spoken as it so often was by salesmen who were doing all the talking and forcing her to listen to figures which she would, usually, rather not hear? Anyway, there was more to her irritation than figures.

A fortnight ago, it had been the back brakes. They had begun to seize up on her way to work, and she had just managed to crawl to College. From there, a breakdown van had, later on, taken her and the maimed car to a nearby garage.

Then, yesterday evening, the same thing happened. This time, it was the front brakes. And the news wasn't good.

How long had they had the little dusky blue Peugeot 205? Over six years, and almost 108,000 miles on the clock. And bodywork that was showing signs of rust. Other repairs would need doing before the MOT, due next January. But that was precisely what Hannah had been hoping: that the car would last till then, till they'd had time to look at others, till her contract was more secure. True, she had taken a test drive in a gleaming new blue-green 106, but with no sense of urgency, just to see.

The one thing she did not want, in the middle of all the rest, was the pressure of deciding to buy another car. But there it was. They would have to do some thinking over the weekend.

You could look at it this way: some people never owned a car. According to a recent study, one-third of British children lived below the poverty line. People were starving all over the world.

You had to keep a sense of proportion … all the same, it was rather inconvenient.

The blue Peugeot 205 which was, at that moment, marooned on a ramp with no brake shoes on, figured prominently in the photo album devoted to the summer of 1988.

'We went to the Alps for our twenty-fifth wedding anniversary,' Hannah would explain to those visitors who, sometimes, flicked distractedly through the pages.

They would reply, 'How lovely!', or words to that effect.

The start hadn't been particularly lovely. They were due to embark from Portsmouth on the night crossing. The preceding weekend, their daughter had gone with a friend to Corfu, on one of those reckless – at least, that's what Hannah called it – flight-only deals. The idea was to save money and rely for accommodation on the locals who, according to the friend, flocked to the airport to offer bed and breakfast to foreigners in exchange for some money. Since then, there had been reports on the radio of some British youths molesting a taxi driver in Majorca. As a result, it was said that the police were cracking down on travellers arriving on the Spanish and Greek islands without accommodation. To crown it all, the phone had rung several times, only to go dead when someone picked it up. Were the girls trying to ring up? Were they in trouble? They couldn't possibly, could they, be in prison?

So, when the day to embark had come, Hannah felt reluctant to leave and therefore sever the possible telephone link. It didn't make for relaxed preparations. Nevertheless, they left for Portsmouth at the appointed time.

Once they had got into the line of cars waiting to board the ferry, she panicked. Refused to go on board and told John to pull up by the side. She shouted at him in anger and distress, in utter frustration because nobody seemed to care. And not only that, but she was made to feel stupid for worrying about worrying things.

Finally, having decided to board after all, she was rude to the official who suggested they took their turn further back in the queue.

Once the car was parked on the lower deck of the ship, they went up to the bar and ordered half a bottle of red wine – which meant Hannah had most of it since John drank very little. Half a bottle wasn't a great deal. But it wasn't very good wine, and it was enough, in the circumstances, to make her feel thick-headed when they landed in Ouistreham in the early hours of the morning, after only a few hours in their cabin and even fewer of sleep – and smarting with remorse at having treated John so badly, at having got so incensed.

They took it slowly along the roads of Normandy, stopping every now and then to stretch their legs or take a catnap.

Towards the end of the morning, Lisieux restored them a little. The basilica was cool and smelt of candle wax. The exhibition on the Carmelite order revived in Hannah, briefly, the occasional longing she had experienced in early adolescence for such a life of dedication. A longing no doubt present in many young Catholic girls, she told herself. A longing which had much to do, probably, with an escapist and mistaken perception of religious life. Nevertheless, the presence of Saint Theresa, a benevolent touch upon her childhood, still retained some calming influence.

Hannah lit a candle in front of her statue and looked up at her. *La petite Sainte Thérèse*, as she was called, to distinguish her from her more formidable counterpart from Avila. *La petite Sainte Thérèse* whose statue, moulded in a special kind of phosphorescent plaster, glowed on the mantelpiece in her parents' house after you turned the lights off. *La petite Sainte Thérèse* who was said to have promised, 'I will spend my time in Heaven showering the earth with roses'.

Hannah bought yet another medal of her in the shop. And, to look after body as well as soul, she made sure to buy a bottle of Calvados from a booth in front of the basilica.

Some three years after that summer, her world having got steadily greyer and her panic attacks more intense and frequent, she had accepted to see a psychotherapist, on the advice of her GP. She had been wary; she had little taste for dives into the subconscious. What she needed was something, someone, to help her live *now.*

As it turned out, this was exactly what was on offer. The therapist wasn't interested in what might have happened in her childhood, although he encouraged her to speak about it if it helped. But his chief goal seemed to help her find out what was preventing her from living now. Starting from that, he would seek, with her, the best way to move on from this point.

Nevertheless, she had recoiled at first from revealing so many of her thoughts to someone whom she did not know. Having agonised about it for a while, and paused the appointment process, she had finally taken the plunge, decided to ask for help, and gone back.

She had not known whether this was wise: the books which list names and their meanings will tell you that Hannah and its derivatives come from a Hebrew word meaning 'wise'. Hannah did not rate her store of wisdom very highly. She could never, as her mother had repeatedly pointed out, do things by halves. She often – too often? – followed her heart.

Was it wise, hence, to trust this unknown person fully? If not fully, would someone please explain to her how you half-trusted a person with some of your most inner thoughts? Surely, you had to decide: you either trusted or you did not. So, she had decided to trust. Nor had her trust been misplaced. If the time ever came when she was left with only one thought about this particular experience, it would be this one: time after time, she had been met with understanding, warmth and patience.

Gradually, she had learnt to talk about what was troubling her, even when she felt 'stupid' about it. She had learnt to take her panics apart and deal with them better. To talk before she reached the boiling point. To communicate with John again. Not to get so frustrated because life was so often uncertain.

And time after time, it was the little blue 205 which had taken her to the hospital where she attended the sessions.

The course of therapy had not always run smoothly. She now recalled some episodes with a certain amusement. Once, the therapist had suggested that she might belong to a category of people he called 'sensation seekers'. She had been indignant. Was he suggesting that she came to the sessions, which cost her a great deal in emotional terms, just in search of cheap thrills?

But when she could bring herself to ask him what he meant, the answer was simply that he was thinking about a recognised category of those who needed excitement as a stimulation to 'functioning' well. Could you really put people in categories? That seemed a bit too simple to Hannah. But if you tolerated this, then she fitted well enough into that category: the one thing she couldn't stand was boredom.

So, yes, overall, the experience had been positive.

But there was a catch. A painful side to it. You could not entrust your life to someone to that degree without becoming in some way dependent on them. And then, you had to leave the support they gave, you had to work things out for yourself.

There were those who said they would rather stay depressed because, with depression, you knew where you were: in a world of grey, where nothing excited you too much, but nothing hurt you too much either. She had lived in such a world. It had not stayed predictably grey, but had gradually grown darker, and the fears had turned into panics. So, she had chosen not to stay in it. She had accepted help.

And now that the world had become, again, colourful or dark in turn, she would have to give up that help; to steer her course through it on her own. That seemed daunting. It was the consequence of getting more able to cope – but the other side of the coin.

As she got better and saw the end of the association getting closer, there was a dull pain in her chest – a pain which no amount of wisdom could dislodge, a pain for which no gratitude for the improvement in her could quite make up. It was a difficult time. A painful time. But she had come through it all, through the ups and downs. She had survived.

She had survived because she knew she had not been abandoned. She had been told that, if she needed to, she could reach out. When she had done so, she had felt supported, even valued. And that, for her who trusted herself so little and so seldom, had been at first a source of wonder, and then a source of strength.

It had been hard at times, but perhaps not as difficult as she had feared. She had, gradually, relearnt old skills. Coped better than expected, most of the time. But not without a lot of heartache, of tears, of soul searching, of episodes of discouragement, after which a new level of acceptance seemed to make the pain softer, easier to bear.

Almost one year after it had come to a close, when she found herself suddenly and unexpectedly reliving those months of transition, they still had the power of making her stop short, catch her breath and smart in the renewed sharpness of loss. They remained in her memory as a curious mixture of episodes, sharp and painful as a knife edge, interspersed with blurred patches to which some kind of imprecise and nagging ache was still attached.

Today was one year to the day since she had left the shelter of the regular meetings. One year to the day since the very last official appointment and all the fear that its anticipation had held at the time. And that day, as during so many others, the little car had been witness to successive, quick moments of fear, relief, grief and elation.

As the anniversary approached, she had prepared herself, Pavlov-dog like, for some bells to be rung and for some reactions to follow. Having prepared herself, she was cautiously relieved to find many reactions less intense than she had feared.

What she had not prepared herself for was the demise of the little blue Peugeot 205, her companion in so many waiting hours and so many aftershocks.

During the weekend, she and John decided to cut their losses. They would buy the 106 Hannah had test-driven. They called the garage on Monday morning and arranged to sign some papers on Wednesday afternoon. The car would be ready at the beginning of next week.

'We've also got to take away what's left in the 205,' said Hannah, after they had signed the documents.

Stupid as it seemed to her, she wanted a few minutes on her own with the old car. It was at the end of the repair area, its wheels back on. There wasn't much to clear. She took a red triangle and a pair of jump leads from the boot. Then she opened the door and sat in the driver's seat. Some cassettes, a couple of old bills, a copy of the insurance documents, an out-of-date book of parking vouchers, a small purse containing change.

She had brought a large plastic bag. As things went into it, she could not help thinking of someone dying in hospital. You go in afterwards, and all you are given is a black plastic bag containing the last remaining vestiges of a presence now gone for ever. An inappropriate, exaggerated analogy? Maybe. But let no one tell her this was just a heap of metal. This was a whole chunk of her life.

As she made to get out, her eye was caught by the corner of a small card wedged at the back of the shelf under the dashboard. She pulled it out. '24-Hour Windscreen Replacement Service'. She froze. Suddenly, she was back in the thick of last summer. Last June. Back in a car park in town where, after she had emerged from one of her darkest sessions, she and John were preparing to get out of the car, thinking, hoping, that a little shopping might be a distraction. Looking out, seeing these seemingly normal, carefree people milling around, she had suddenly and savagely been hit by the incongruity of going shopping. By the impossibility of getting her life back in order. By the utter futility of it all. She hated them all for being so normal. She hated herself for not being like them. She couldn't breathe.

Somehow, she had to let out some of that despair. Otherwise, she felt she was going to choke. And she had head-butted the windscreen until she was vaguely aware of John pulling her back. Only then did she realise that she had cracked the glass. She felt no physical pain, and had done herself no serious damage. But inside, she felt something adrift, something like a shipwreck. And she was terrified.

As she saw it now, that was when she may well have hit rock-bottom. It probably was one of the turning points. In the early days of therapy, she had imagined that, if the treatment worked, there would be one dramatic turning point only; some kind of blinding flash on the road to Damascus, leading to a resolution of her inner conflicts once and for all. She now knew the turning points to be many, and each resolution to be tentative. But it was from that episode onwards that she had begun to crawl forward, with the help of some good people: her therapist, her husband, her GP, a couple of true friends.

On the day she was due to pick up the new car, she woke early in a panic. Was this the right decision? Was she merely going to add even worse pollution to the world their children and grandchildren would inhabit after she was dead? Should they have only one car? Should they have decided to have the brakes repaired on the 205? She wanted to call the garage and say, 'I've changed my mind. Repair the brakes. Do the bodywork. Put in a new engine when this one is dead. Do *anything*, but *please, please, please*, don't put it on the scrap heap.' She wanted her little car back. She wanted that chunk of her life back.

It was late afternoon when she finally drove the blue-green 106 out of the garage.

'Well,' said the censorious small voice that was apt to intrude upon what she called her meaner thoughts. 'Well, the last time you drove this, it was just a bit of a dream. Now it's yours. Shouldn't you feel a bit more elated?'

The hospital was only a short distance from the garage. She hesitated, then turned into the long drive of the former asylum, which led to the sun-baked brick buildings. Trees, shrubs, large expanses of lawn. No doubt the administrators and financiers, in their merciless drive for efficiency and profit, would have most of it pulled down. The red-brick tower which rose on the horizon, which made her think of some Constable painting with

Dedham church silhouetted in the distance, was likely to escape destruction. It was, she believed, listed and hence protected. But, more important for the company who would buy and develop the site, it was the base of multiple mobile phone antennae.

Hannah stopped as close to the tower as she could. 'I'm bringing you here,' she told the new car, 'so that you get the feel of the place. Your predecessor brought me here regularly. You won't have to do that. But this place has been – it still is – part of my life. Part of me. So, you might as well be aware it exists.'

The car park was half empty. She sat, still, in the shade of a tree, on the right of the main building. She put one of the cassettes she had brought into the deck: *Simon Boccanegra*. A complicated plot she could never remember, but that didn't matter. What mattered was that the emotions came through. That's what mattered. That's why she loved opera. For the intensity of the emotions. The characters could give full vent to their feelings. They didn't always have to hold back. To be always two steps behind the full measure of their passions – love, fear, anger, longing. Yes, she heard all the arguments against such extremes: surely, it was a bit over the top? Surely, if Violetta was really dying of consumption, she wouldn't be able to sing so much and so loud? So, the world of opera was implausible? Impossible? Pretty impossible, too, at times, the demands of an ordinary life. It was a relief to have an occasional and vicarious respite from those demands.

She wiped her tears and looked around. It was a peaceful place in the late afternoon sun. There was a lot to be thankful for, but what she found most difficult was the fickleness of her moods. She often chided herself for this, she often goaded herself into remembering that, at least as far as she knew, she wasn't harbouring a terminal illness; that she wasn't in a refugee camp or about to be butchered by some neighbouring guerrillas. And indeed, on some days, an hour in the garden, a leisurely meal or a good swim at the pool made her feel that life could be simple and pleasurable.

What she found intolerable on other days was not to have a defined goal, a strong, inner flame to which she could turn for reassurance and comfort. She missed a sense of urgency, a sense of purpose. Depending on the colour of the day, she would despair and wonder whether the inner light she remembered could ever burn so fiercely again. On better days, she knew it was still there, alive, flickering and ready to leap up. She had, in any case, learnt to deal with these changes of mood in the course of the treatment. If you don't have a long-term goal, create at least a short-term one and get on with it. It made sense. It often worked, sometimes well.

But it was futile to pretend that the two kinds of purpose – passion versus stoicism? – were the same. She knew both and she knew the difference.

The bureaucrats and the promoters might decide to pull this place down and build yet another residential park of characterless houses. In the meantime, it stood as witness to an important part of her life. More than that, it had been a haven, a sanctuary; it had given her a time to pause. But it couldn't be a substitute for life.

She couldn't quite put it clearly in her mind, but it was something like this: you couldn't turn places into absolutes; or people. It was all too easy to take a place and build it into some kind of earthly paradise. Too easy to take someone's perfection in the area of their life you meet, transfer it to all the other areas of their life which you do not know, and make this person into some sort of ideal. Too easy to want to hold on to that. Too easy to demand permanence.

Perhaps there were few permanent havens? Perhaps there were few permanently perfect people? Yet she knew, absolutely, that there were some wonderful havens and some wonderful people you might meet through life; she knew these were exceptional. But you could not lay any claim to them, for what made them special was a gift; the gift of their presence, which was the result of their freedom. Throughout life, if you were lucky enough to encounter such havens and such people, you would be grateful for the blessings they could bestow. But blessings, being gifts, could not be demanded. As with everything in life which no amount of wishing could hold still – seasons, light, shadow, time – blessings were gifts granted only to those not trying in vain to hold them prisoners.

She suddenly saw, as clearly as if it had been pasted on the windscreen, a poster she had stuck on her wall when she was – was she even twenty? Seagulls flying over the waves, and printed on the sky, the words, 'If you love something, let it go. If it comes back, it's yours. If it doesn't, it never was.' She remembered feeling slightly light-headed when she had discovered the poster in a bookshop – a little like drinking a glass of strong red wine on an empty stomach. How wisdom could go to your head if you did not have to apply it! In her more mature years, when she had found it necessary to live by that beautiful saying, she had discovered it to be harder than she'd expected.

If only understanding could erase the pain, she thought. But why should it? How could it? She knew her heart needed time; time to rally round to the conclusions her mind reached – and often after inner struggles. She knew how hard that time could be to live through.

A price to pay? She also knew the gifts she had received to be worth it.

She gently turned down the music, took the cassette out and put it away in its box. She leaned back against the headrest and closed her eyes, listening to the silence. Joy and pain, love and loss, light and darkness, the fleeting and the eternal – all so tightly interwoven. When she opened her eyes again, the leaves of a nearby lime tree cast, in turn, pale sunlight and shadows across the windscreen. Words she had recently seen on a sundial came back to her: 'Lux & Umbra vicissim, sed semper Amor'.[36]

She started the car, reversed it and drove home.

Two hours later, the phone rang. It was Jean, their next-door neighbour. 'I'm going into town tomorrow morning. I wondered whether you needed anything. Or do you want a lift?'

'Thank you, but we've just bought another car. It's kind of you to offer.'

'Oh good. And are you pleased with it?'

---

36 'Light and shadow in turn, but always love.'

'Yes, yes, it's a little 106. You can see it if you look out of your bedroom window. It looks very nice. It should save a lot of hassle, as it's unlikely to break down for a while!'

'Sounds wonderful. I'm so glad you've got your life sorted out.'

'You might very well say that,' thought Hannah. But she just replied, 'Thank you. And for the offer of shopping. I'll see you soon.'

She put the phone down. Jean was a kind soul, always ready to offer help.

She looked out of the window. The little blue-green 106 was standing in the drive. Cedar green, the catalogue called it. Nice name. Nice car.

Yes, it was a nice little car. But for now, it was just a nice little stranger.

> *First drafted 1995, in homage and gratitude to B. – and to the Graylingwell that was, a place where sanctuary could be found for a while. Re-wrought 2023-2024 in gratitude for the light of C., a special beacon in my life, and for the sanctuary he offers.*

WORDS - HOME AND WORK

Someone asked me recently, 'How would you describe your personality?'

I had not given much thought to a definition, and the question sent me, once more, after some words I could use. Hence my foray into etymology. The following words all have to do, or so it seems to me, with our relations with others and with our status in the society we live in.

First

Amiable: from Late Latin *amicabilis* via Old French.
Congenial: from the combined Latin *com/con* + *genialis* = of
   birth, kindred.
Egregious: (this one I find particularly interesting;
   especially in modern English – which always takes
   me by surprise, as I have to remember it is not a
   compliment!) It is related to *gregarious*, as it is from
   grex = flock, but here it means 'out of the flock',
   which could be exceptionally good or bad. In Italian,
   it has kept the positive sense, whereas it has come to
   mean the reverse in English – how and when? The
   OED says:

> The first appearance of 'egregious' in English was around 1550 … But 'egregious' was also used sarcastically in Latin, and in about 1566.

While Merriam-Webster tells us:

> egregious was … apparently arising as an ironic use, to mean conspicuously bad or wrong, blatant, flagrant.

Gregarious: from the Latin *grex, greg = flock*. Seventeenth century: of animals living in flocks, or plants growing in open clusters.
Private: from Latin *privus* = single, individual.
Sociable: from the Latin *socius* = companion.
Solitary: from Latin *solus* = alone.

This passion for words is nothing new. But this quest has made me think of the way I relate to others in everyday life – to family, friends and work.

I have been at ease, throughout life, with the persona I adopt in teaching. Concentrated teaching for residential weekends, brief but intense and demanding, with even meal times often taken over by those who wish to speak French all the time.

Teaching spread over one or several years is more relaxed when no exam is scheduled. Teaching with the Open University through distance learning – their speciality – and through meetings, day schools, and summer school one year. Teaching international students at the British campus of an American College for many years.

Of individual students I have fewer memories. Those pushed through my door by parents anxious about exam results were never endearing because they did not want to be there.

A few others have left lasting memories, and one still enjoys an hour's French every now and then. Such individual students are so rewarding. And so has been an especially long-term association with my Midhurst group; I have known some of its members for many years, first through the WEA, then privately.

Since I also function well as a student in a small group, I am sociable, if anyone is in need of a label; and often but not always, depending on personalities, gregarious as an active member of a small professional group. My best experiences, in the many courses I have taught, have been connected to the length or the intensity of the connection between the students and myself.

I have enjoyed many weekends devoted to practising a language through literature, which often built up over the years, as at Maryland College for instance. For many years this College, on the outskirts of Woburn, was dedicated to weekend or short-term courses for adults. I first went there as a student on a Creative Writing course. Having chatted with Alex (the VP) at coffee times, I was asked whether I would be interested in 'team-teaching' with him on books the BBC was glancing at in a programme called,

I believe, 'Six novels from France in translation'. These novels marked the first of many such weekends I spent at Maryland, exploring the treasures of French literature with students and becoming firm friends with Alex and his wife Josefina. Their friendship soon extended to our family and they stayed with us, and we with them, over the years.

I may have had the very best of adult education at Maryland, but I also taught in similar establishments: Wansfell College, on the outskirts of London, was friendly but lacked the cohesion given to Maryland by Alex's presence; Missenden Abbey, beautifully set on the edge of the Chiltern Hills, focused more intensely on corporate entertainment and week-long courses. This was their main source of income and could make us feel like the *parents pauvres* at the weekend, when material and equipment might work – or not.

There was, in those weekend courses, the feeling that a dozen of us were living a privileged fraction of time. We may have been different in our respective everyday lives but, for this short span, we were all focused on one text, one author and on life seen through them. We had one common goal: to exchange our thoughts on these by means of a foreign language. To exchange our views of life.

It reminded me of Boccaccio's *Decameron*, set in a time of plague, when ten young people seek refuge in the hills above Florence and, for a short while, banish the outside world and the pestilence. In their retreat, they spend time sharing stories, food and thoughts, respecting rules of courtesy. Thus they create, for a while, a world of their own. This world is only temporary and all know it. At the end of the tenth day, they make their way back into the city, just as my students and I made our way back to everyday life – a transition which did not always prove instantly easy.

The many weekends spent at Maryland College were the result of one serendipitous encounter. Those years of teaching near home also started seemingly by chance.

One of my evening students at a Chichester College French class had a full-time job near Arundel, at the British Campus of a New Hampshire College. Their French tutor having taken a sabbatical, my student asked me whether I would be happy to replace her for the next two semesters. She never came back (I occasionally hear her on Radio 4), and I stayed some 17 years, teaching French to start with, then gradually adding Italian and Art History.

Those years, too, were happy. The student population on the British Campus of New England College came from all over the world, not just the US, as many Middle Eastern families sought to give their sons and daughters some US education and felt safer sending them to Europe rather than to the US campus.

We also had US students coming to experience a season or two of English theatre and museums; these students made the most of what treasures London contains. With them, we had so-called field-trips to London for the day; the expression caused perplexity for some of the support staff, seeing me dressed for town and wondering how I would cope with a trip in the open countryside without the robust gear needed to wander through hill and vale. Such trips might be to see an exhibition or visit famous places that perfectly illustrated some architectural features in our course.

It was also my privilege to teach students from Lithuania and Latvia, as one of our colleagues was Lithuanian and arranged a partnership. It was a great joy to share what knowledge I had with these young people avid for the experience, to see their keenness and love of the arts, their eagerness to draw everything they could from these few months abroad.

I also valued belonging to the Open University, with whom I started teaching French when New England College closed in 1996 (to my great sorrow and that of many staff members). The OU has existed for years, and had such an advantage over many other universities during the endless months of lockdown, when students were deprived of their rightful access to tuition and social life.

I enjoyed teaching with the institution, meeting the students in evening classes, working with some colleagues to prepare and give a Saturday School. The Summer School which took place every year proved immensely enjoyable when I was able to stay on the campus of Caen University in the summer of 1999, working in turn as tutor and adviser.

As time went on, the marking and interaction increasingly shifted towards the internet and, although I still found my job valuable, I missed the more frequent contact with students.

One of the great benefits of teaching with the OU was that tutors also had access to students' experiences, being able to study a course in their own time. I collected a few and enjoyed the opportunity!

Last but not least, my Midhurst–Fernhurst group. This, as Maryland and New England College, started via serendipity – and Creative Writing. Having decided to write my memories of early life (as our first grandson was born), I attended a WEA course once a week. Pam, the tutor, knew I liked Proust. About half-way through the course, she asked me whether I would be willing to replace the Midhurst tutor for the rest of the term, as he was ill. Alas for him, he did not recover – and I stayed, first teaching at The Grange in Midhurst for a number of years, then in the houses of some members who wanted to carry on when 'too low' numbers would have closed the class.

The group did indeed become smaller, as people moved away, fell ill or acquired grandchildren. But the small group that was left has been among the most enriching I have come across in my long years spent teaching. We reluctantly ended our meetings in autumn 2024, but have kept in contact through infrequent but meaningful emails. Some thoughts from former students keep my courage up when needed.

From one, after a review of a few books: 'I mention only some of the books which have meant the most to me but am forever grateful for having been introduced to such a variety of writers. I have so enjoyed our time together, with good friends and discussions.'

From another: 'It was also a profound empathy which allowed us to reflect on so many different situations and relationships and thus enrich our lives. You encouraged and facilitated this enrichment and for this I am truly grateful.'

I have always known that this book group gave me at least as much as I gave them, sometimes more, and thus feel so truly and deeply rewarded by such messages.

Back to gregariousness.

I am also gregarious on family occasions. Whenever some of us come together for a celebration, or solely for the pleasure of being together, I rejoice at the warmth of the occasion.

This was greatly emphasised when we were able to meet again after the long months of seclusion due to Covid. I do remember, in particular, the very first of these meetings at our elder son and family's home. It was so very special to be sitting round the table, all eight of us, without the worry of further enforced imprisonment and separation. Over those months of lockdown, I kept notes of the dates when we had last been able to hug sons, daughter, partners, grandchildren and friends. Rereading them is heartbreaking: so many days, weeks, months lost; they will never come back. And so tragic for many as they were not able to bid farewell to their loved ones, a wound made worse by the conviction some had that the lockdowns had been the cause of death rather than a tragic coincidence.

Unlike my parents, grandmothers and godmother, who saw one another daily at some periods of their lives, we do not meet weekly or even more often. But when we do, it is indeed special.

Special too have been some holidays with grandchildren. One of these was in Wales, in a caravan, where we stayed for a week with Alastair and Dominic, our daughter's sons. We weren't sure they would weather being separated from their parents for a number of days in a place they did not know, since all other such separations had been at our house, which they knew well. So, we promised (to them and to Claire and Max, their parents) that we would take them home if they so wished. Fortunately, this turned out not to be necessary, hence we made the most of our time together. Among the visits I remember are those to a Dinosaur Park, Ramsey Island and a chocolate factory. Although some of these were somewhat strange and did not quite live up to our expectations, it was the spirit we entered into them that made them worth the visit. We concluded every day by watching Tom and Jerry cartoons together.

This seems such a long time ago, now that they both are young adults. Whereas Alastair's practical nature is reflected in the hours of volunteering he and his wife give to St John Ambulance, his passion for traditions and history inspires pastimes as diverse as heraldry and steam trains. Dominic, firmly anchored in the cyberworld through his work, is also sensitive to the world of imagination since he met his girlfriend through theatre when both, as backstage crew, were helping to create 'The cloud-capp'd towers, the gorgeous palaces'.[37]

It is such a long time since that holiday, and yet it has come to be part of family lore, and is still remembered fondly.

Other memorable holidays were in Brittany. During some of the long summer months, Chris and I went to Ploubalay, not far from St Malo, before François could be free from work; this meant that while enjoying a change of scene, we could also give a hand to Sarah when it came to entertaining, changing and feeding four youngsters!

Ploubalay was to them as Mabs' cottage in Derbyshire was to our own children: a haven separated from everyday life during the long summer months. But the year when they all joined us in Finistère also stands out as different and special. We took walks by the coast, visited a nearby harbour and, back at the house, watched *Joseph and The Amazing Technicolor Dreamcoat* on a videotape available in the 'library'. We watched it so many times that Annabelle and her triplet siblings almost knew the songs by heart, and we all ended up singing them!

As their cousins, all four have grown up. All seem to have a sense of adventure. Annabelle works in the City.

---
[37] William Shakespeare, *The Tempest*, IV, 1, 152

She loves playing netball, visiting bookshops and reading. Whenever possible, she travels, often with friends. Giselle is a much-valued paediatric nurse in London; she has used some of her holidays to venture far, volunteering in the Dominican Republic and in Costa Rica. Benedict, whose love of performing goes back many years, has just been accepted on a post-graduate acting course. Both he and Jacques compose and sing; Jacques also plays the guitar; they make the music available through various channels, which to me – still attached to my CD collection – could be a closed world if I did not pursue its access because I would like to share these young people's experiences!

Our youngest grandchildren, though, have not yet grown up – an interesting point, since our son Nicholas is Claire's twin brother; whereas Claire's elder son Alastair is our oldest grandchild, Nick and Tori's daughter Oona is the youngest. Her two brothers are older. Link, the oldest, is seven; slightly built (though with hidden strength), he is sensitive and artistic. Océan, now five, has had nicknames alluding to his robust physique and his fearless tendency to dive into any activity. Oona, at three, can resist her brothers with a stern franglais, 'No! Pas ça!'; at other times, she loves mothering and organising them. All three demand much time, which is shared as evenly as possible by their parents.

They have an older half-brother Oscar, Tori's son, who studies computer science in Annecy; he is our 'honorary' grandson.

We joined them once in Tignes, where they spend the skiing season as Tori is a ski instructor and the children ski as naturally as they walk. In the summer they move to southwest France, and we stayed near them several times, so that we could join them in day trips.

One year, when Claire was with us, we enjoyed a feast in the forest near their home to celebrate joint birthdays, a themed feast with animal costumes. We went to a reserve teeming with wild life. We took walks along beaches, had lunches in the sunshine, and went to San Sebastian for the day, admiring some magnificent views of the Pyrénées on the way. We spent a few delightful hours in Bayonne, and went into the beautiful cathedral after sharing a lunch in its shadow.

Cathedrals are special places to me, when I think of the engineering marvels, of all the hands that built them centuries ago; when I perceive the echo of so many prayers around me; when I light a candle in thanksgiving and petition.

Such occasions ensure that, even though we do not live next door to any of our grandchildren, they still know us better than their parents may have known the majority of the older generations.

At the time of writing, it concerns me that those who live furthest away in France, and who are also the youngest, will not have as much time to get to know us as their older cousins have done. It saddens me that we do not meet so often. They will not have as long as their cousins to build up a store of memories – but we can only deal with the situations life gives us.

Whether they live near or far, those in our close family, our children and grandchildren, have often given me courage, strength and hope when needed. Their love makes life's trials easier to face, and life's joys more intense.

Having looked at my reactions to various situations I have come to the conclusion that, in Jungian terms, I am an extroverted introvert: ready to invest time and energy with people who mean a lot to me, enjoying such times. Often needing time to recover from the energy spent on these occasions. And also seeking solitude rather than the company of strangers for the sake of it.

Why do I need a name for my natural bent? Is it because I feel I have to justify myself? Do I have to make excuses for the many times I do not feel particularly sociable? In the end, no one probably fits one label exactly – very likely, we are all on a 'spectrum'. Whatever name we seek for our personality, how do we balance family and work? Do we need anything more to feel that life is worth living?

It seems to me that we all need more than daily life: the life of work, the life of family – however good these may be. Whether we are part of a network through our profession, or through our relatives, we are also, and always, ourselves. Our younger son often quotes the advice on plane journeys, 'If masks are needed, they will drop from their place. Put yours on first – you can help no one unless you are safe yourself.'

I have loved many teaching jobs I have done. I love my family deeply. But I also need another dimension, one from which I can draw strength, inspiration and momentum to give back to others. This could be a well-established or a new acquaintance, a deep, long-held conviction or a newly discovered philosophy, the pursuing of a challenging process – something which keeps the flame of life burning bright.

None of these, in any way, diminishes the love I have for my close family. Indeed, does it not make me the holder of more riches to share with them? Yet, the cost of these increased riches for me may also make me more difficult to live with.

Be that as it may, this is me, and I can only be true to my own self, as Polonius advises us to be.

CHICHESTER WALLS

Seasons

Do the Chichester Walls house the souls of former Roman inhabitants? The Roman city goes back to the first century AD, when it was known as *Noviomagus*. According to local sources, the walls with gates in the four cardinal points date from c. 300 AD. These walls are no longer complete and the gates and the towers have mainly disappeared. But the very plan of the city – with its main arteries named North Street, South Street, West Street and East Street – still bears witness to its Roman foundation.

After the Romans left the city, around 400 AD, the walls fell into disrepair and had to wait for restoration to begin in the 1370s. Sizeable portions still remain, some easily accessible by foot, especially in the two northern quadrants. The northeast section was altered in the eighteenth century to make a shady walk within the walls. Tree roots, according to local historians, caused some damage, which had to be repaired, but the visible part of the parapet is mediæval and rests upon the Roman core.[38] We can therefore say that we are stepping into the footprints of our Roman ancestors, made over twenty centuries ago.

---

[38] *The City of Chichester*, Chichester City Council, 1967, 18th edition.

It is because of this distant past that I wonder whether some of the souls of those who built, lived and traded within these walls have left traces in their flint and lime core. Whether they have or not, I am convinced that some of my soul will be found in them long after I have gone.

I have walked there so often, especially on the north quadrants. When walking westwards on the northeast wall, I have often stopped above the remains of a motte-and-bailey, with a play area below. In February, I have paused and gazed long at a most beautiful mimosa tree, in the back garden of one of the tightly packed terraced houses, lined up along Franklin Place. It must have been there many years, judging from its majestic size. From the top of the wall, you can see it so close. Not quite close enough to catch its heavenly scent, but close enough to see the myriad small golden balls tightly packed into sprays, plumes of beauty giving their light even on rainy days. And there have been plenty of these as I begin to write this at the very end of February 2025.

Fortunately, even the capricious weather has not stunted this beautiful tree, according to the photographs I've received. Two years ago, it never quite flowered. One branch seemed to be struggling, and it must have affected the growth of the whole. Even last year, you could still see this greener spray just beginning to flower, while the rest of the tree had generously given its wonderful sight to passers-by for many days. In April, I walked there many times and did not, at first, recognise my dear mimosa. It had been severely pruned, which

I hoped would do it good for the following spring. It seems to have done.

The walls are blessed with a succession of flowerings. After the magnificence of the mimosa, at the beginning of April comes the fragile, fleeting wild cherry, a young slender tree planted just at the northeast entrance to the walls. So beautiful, so brief. I love its delicate branches, its all-too-soon fading white blossom. All it means about transience and the precious beauty of special moments, friendship, life … I find it achingly wonderful.

As the year unfolds, the trees get fuller. Soon it will be June, and June has been, for many years, associated with both linden trees and the marking of A-level papers. Incongruous companions? Possibly, but they have been, for me, concurrent for many years. Past the middle of May, I begin to follow the progress of these lime trees as I walk on or outside the walls. They are fully in leaf and, in-between, I can see the nascent flowers, which will envelop us in their heady perfume, but for such a brief time. I keep watch as I do not want to miss one minute of their short-lived flowering.

I did not miss any of it last year. I missed none of their subtle yet pervading scent. Whether from the south walls down towards a path along the river Lavant, or along the northwest walls, I fully breathed in their beauty. Was this a premonition that it might be the last time I could do so? As I first wrote this last February, it was painful to think I might not be able to see them unfold this coming summer.

Yet, as I write this now in mid-June, I have just renewed my acquaintance with these limes. It feels like a miracle when I re-read those lines, written six months ago

– lines weighed down by a valediction. But I have seen and breathed in the limes in flower again, and such a miracle has taught me to appreciate more intensely such delights as are given us through nature, love and friendship.

On one of my recent walks in late June, I came across a woman sweeping from the pavement in front of her house something which looked like gold dust. I looked up and, sure enough, tall limes on the opposite side of the road were releasing their pale, fading yellow blossoms; they floated down gently, this ethereal powder of linden flowers, which I was blessed to witness in all their glory only one week before. Seeing these sent me back to one of my favourite passages in a book that divides the calendar into seventy-two seasons, according to the Japanese tradition:

> The messy riot of this point in the year may hold within it the inevitability of death and decay, but deeper still there is rebirth and new potential.[39]

This 'point in the year' is infinitely fleeting. Soon another follows, also bringing change. In truth, even though some particularly marked changes spell out transition to us, I do not believe that times of transition following static times truly exist. Transition goes on all the time. The cells in our body keep on shedding and being renewed. Trees, flowers, nature in general, all follow a similar pattern. Or perhaps, put more simply: in any form of life, stasis is an illusion.

Life is movement.

---
39 Jaines et al., *Nature's Calendar: the British Year in 72 seasons*, 27 June–1 July, p.171.

The succession of seasons is but another illustration of this. It is already shortly past mid-summer and, after a particularly long dry spell, some leaves are showing singed edges. Later in the year, we will watch summer turning into autumn. We shall be blessed by the warmth of the colours: first the horse chestnuts turning into their rich tints; then, the beeches and maples – such a bounty of golden or red shades which come down to lay a bright carpet under our feet, when we are lucky enough to walk upon it.

My students from the United States, who mostly came from the East Coast, used to tell me I just didn't know what fall colours were like. Perhaps they were right, if they drew a direct comparison, but I find plenty to delight me here.

Particularly majestic are the holm oaks along the Avenue de Chartres, although there is a bitter aftertaste to their beauty. At the foot of one of them a plaque states: 'On 1st January 1993, Chichester City Council planted 12 oak trees along the Avenue de Chartres to mark the start of the European Single Market.' Former times, alas.

And when all the leaves have fallen, there will be the beauty of the still, bare branches, etched against the sky; the seemingly lifeless silhouettes poised between earth and heaven. Lifeless? Not if we look closely, for within the branches we shall soon detect the shape of buds pushing themselves towards the light. Reassurance. The endless cycle of decay, growth and rebirth. The promise of life.

February–June 2025

'SUCH STUFF AS DREAMS ARE MADE ON'

A novella

FLIGHT

The taxi dropped Giulia at the door of the North Terminal. She had pre-booked her bags, so she would have time for a coffee before boarding started.

As she sat in one of the cafés, she remembered the first time she had been to Florence. One spring day, just before Easter, on a quest for seeing the art works she had been studying for two years. Works which looked flat on the photographs and yet, if they were buildings or sculptures, demanded to be seen in three dimensions. She remembered the card she had sent to James, a card full of excitement at finding the true impact of these sculpted pillars; these figures she had so often pored over in her books; these figures of which he had spoken so eloquently to her. She remembered his curt answer, thanking her for her 'over-emotional' card from Florence. She should have been warned, so early in their acquaintance.

The board announcing departures clicked, interrupting her thoughts. Letters in a jumble took a while to settle on the right line, forming the names of cities and airports, and she saw her flight announced as *Boarding*. Time to walk along endless corridors, along moving walkways, and find the gate. She would have the leisure to reminisce during the flight.

She had pre-booked a seat, and made sure she sat half over a wing – just to be able to see the earth tilt as the plane changed course soon after take-off. That was one of the great pleasures of flying. Indeed, it was not so much flying she loved, since so often you were over cloud banks, but the take-off and the landing. The take-off most of all: the mounting roar, the increasing power of the engines, the brief stop … then the gathering speed and the feeling of the reaction lift as the runway began to slip away. She couldn't help noticing her neighbour, a priest who did not seem to share her elation, as he repeatedly crossed himself.

The criss-cross railway lines, the motorway, the pattern of carparks, houses and fields, disappeared, swallowed up by clouds. She settled in her seat and closed her eyes. Her mind went back to James. To two weeks ago, helping Rebecca to tidy up his papers. That folder. That impersonal surname, her surname – not the kind of heading you'd give to a friend's correspondence.

She was, again, wondering. Surely, she could not just have imagined his affection, his regard, during all these years? Surely, she had not misread him so totally, so utterly? Yes, he was prone to changes of mood. Yes, she had had to learn to sense them and, when they happened, to keep her distance. They were, she thought, brought on by associations with his daughter, whom he had lost when she was only twenty-five.

As the combined purr of engines and the noise of conversation blended into the background, she leant back against her seat and closed her eyes. Her mind shot back to the beginning of their association.

They had met for the first time, some eight years ago, in the great hall of Newton College, a distance-learning institution based in Cambridge and set up to help, through tutoring by post, students who could devote only part of their time to their chosen studies. The prospectus offered a vast range of subjects, from O levels to degrees, each with the possibility of getting 'remote' help from tutors. James had been a tutor with the College for over ten years, while she had just joined it. Thus, he had introduced her to the methods and ways favoured by the directors regarding distance learning.

'Why Giulia?' James had asked when they first met. 'Why the Italian spelling Gi?'

'My maternal grandmother was called Julie. My mother loved Italy and all things Italian. It was easy to cross the border from the Savoie where we lived. So, she thought she would adopt the Italian spelling for me.'

Since James also knew some of Italy, this had been a common point between them and had eased their first contact. And he, particularly fond of Ronsard, was familiar with Petrarch's sonnets, which she loved. He had also introduced her to some of Michelangelo's poetry.

Then, they had talked about the College and its rules, its customs. James, a former barrister, was English with a French PhD. She, French through her mother and living in France, had spoken the language from birth. Through her mother's obsession with all things Italian and the proximity of Northern Italy, she also had a fair knowledge of Italian. Because of James' experience and seniority, she had asked him to explain what her role would require: what kind of tutoring the College expected, what kind of feedback to give the students.

They did not meet often, but fairly regularly. First, there were the biannual staff meetings at Newton College. These were good because they allowed colleagues who would never have met otherwise to discuss points connected with helping students via correspondence. For these reunions, lodgings were provided for those who travelled from afar. James, having studied at Clare College, had friends in Cambridge and stayed with them. Giulia used the accommodation provided in Homerton College, southeast of the Botanical Gardens and next door to Newton College. She loved staying there. The rooms were long and narrow, almost spartan and rather cell-like, but with the luxury of a small shower en-suite and, if you were lucky enough to be housed in the right wing, wonderful views over the surrounding park, its lawns and trees. From there, it was an easy walk to the Botanical Gardens, and she and James would occasionally do such a walk at lunch time or after meetings. There was also the maze-like treasure trove of Heffer's Bookshop, closer to the city centre.

Apart from these meetings, they found it useful to coordinate some points of their teaching and some common problems they encountered in student essays. James specialised in Mediæval and Renaissance writers, she in those of the eighteenth and nineteenth centuries. However, they were familiar with each other's area of study. Although they taught different modules, they shared some students and it was important to present some coherence in the way assignments were marked and commented upon. They met in London for such exchanges, since James was a Londoner and the University Senate House had a pleasant refectory.

At the beginning of their acquaintance, their conversations were limited to students, their essays, the poets they studied and, occasionally, Italy. Soon, they began to exchange a little more personal information, which was when he had told her about his daughter, Giovanna, a beautiful and promising young lady – killed in a car accident when she was only twenty-five.

As they got to know each other she noticed he had a rather perplexing habit of suddenly shifting from the very personal to the neutral, the purely professional. He might, for instance, recite some lines by Ronsard looking into her eyes as if he were speaking to her:

> *Le temps s'en va, le temps s'en va, ma Dame*
> *Las, le temps non, mais nous nous en allons*
> *Et tôt serons étendus sous la dalle …*
> *Pour ç'aimez-moi cependant qu'êtes belle !*[40]

To his fondness for the sonnets of Michelangelo and Petrarch, he added a great love for some of the pre-Dante poets. Guido Guinizelli, in particular, whom he quoted most often, again looking straight at her. For instance:

---

[40] 'Time is going, time is going my Lady, / Alas, time, no – but we are / And soon will be laid under our gravestones … / and thus, love me whilst you are beautiful!' (Ronsard, from one of the sonnets to Marie Dupin, c. 1555).

Vedut'ho la lucente stella diana,
c'ha preso forma di figura umana;[41]

Having spoken the lines with such intensity – or so it seemed – he would then abruptly change register, give a wry laugh and, shifting his gaze away from her, muse aloud on what was, he said, his main problem – a problem that kept him awake at night, apparently – on how to render sixteenth-century French into English without sounding as if he were plagiarising Robert Herrick. It was difficult indeed, since both Ronsard and Herrick had written about flowers no sooner open than they died, both had taken that image to urge some beautiful woman to make the most of her youth by falling into their arms, and plagiarising was not an issue in their times.

Whether his problems with language were so preoccupying as to keep him awake or not, he still had the eloquence of a barrister and so he had inspired her to study further the relation of Michelangelo's sculpture to his poetry.

Again, one of his letters came back to her. It had brought one of the unfinished marble statues to life for her: 'Such a powerful figure, Giulia, this giant, his head still half-encased in the block of marble, for ever fighting its crushing weight … a bit like us when we can't quite see how to get out of a noose.' It was just like James, and she had got used to this habit of speaking, or writing, in riddles. To use language to reveal or to hide? There was no way of knowing whether the above remark was just a

---

41 'I have seen the star of the morning, Venus, / She has taken human form;' (Guido Guinizelli, second half of the thirteenth century).

general comment on life, or whether he was referring to problems he perceived between Giulia and himself.

Whatever his intentions, his eloquence (which, she had reminded herself, may have been only the eloquence of the barrister), his eloquence was such that she had to see these figures when she first went to Florence: to see Michelangelo's *Slaves* in the Accademia Gallery; to step into the library and the memorial chapel to the young Medici, which he had designed for the church of San Lorenzo. It had truly been breathtaking to step into these spaces, to stand in front of these marble giants. It had seemed so natural to share these emotions with James in a brief postcard – only for it to be slighted. Perplexing – again.

She must have dozed off. As she looked out of the porthole, she saw sharp, snowy needles against the sky, now clear. They were over the Alps, a sight she remembered so vividly from her first flight to Pisa, after mist had dispelled and the summits had suddenly seemed to shoot out of the sky as if they were coming towards her at speed. Beautiful. It still made her catch her breath.

A small orange bell lit up above the seats. A message came over the PA system, 'Fasten your seat belts, we will soon begin the descent towards Pisa.'

FLORENCE

Giulia got up.

'Marvellous coffee, thank you!'

Signora Cappelli smiled. 'So glad you enjoy it every morning! I wish you a pleasant day.'

Giulia set off through the park of the *pensione*. As she picked her way over the uneven stones of the path, she could feel the sun, already warm, on her back. She lifted her face to meet a gentle breeze so unlike the wind she had left at Heathrow, which had made her relegate to the back of her wardrobe the light coat she had worn to leave home.

She reached the gate and stopped, looking around. That other scent, stronger than all the rest … pines. A row of them descended the avenue to her right and the fragrance was already strong. Too soon for the cones to open, releasing pine nuts with a dry crack. Too soon to join the people who came with paper bags to collect these precious nuts and take them home. But the promise was there.

As she walked down the avenue, traffic rumbled past on the cobbles, splashing waves of sound at her. When she reached Porta Romana, traders were propping up crates of fruit and greens on the pavement, the bright mounds of strawberries and the dark green of watermelon skins contrasting with pyramids of pale vine peaches. Early crops from the south, no doubt, as was the bunch of dark grapes she chose from a stall.

The trader, whom she had got to know a little during the past few days, smiled at her. 'And where is the Signora off to today?'

'I'm just off to the Carmine.'

'Ah! You'll like it. Beautiful church.'

The Florentine accent transformed 'chiesa' into 'hiesa', the h guttural like the Spanish *jota*. It made her smile, despite having heard it so many times – not something course books could teach you!

Still smiling, she stepped into the road to cross the square. She had to jump back in haste to avoid a Vespa driven by a young man, his open shirt and long hair flying in the wind. Not for the likes of him, helmets, boots, tight-fitting safety gear. Freedom was what they craved, even if it was the freedom to kill themselves or anyone crossing their path. She stepped back further and waited for a gap between two swarms of fast riders.

She was now following part of the old walls, along a wide avenue bordered with plane trees. A sign on the side of a house caught her eye: Piazza Torquato Tasso. Tasso, she sighed. Tasso and his love poetry, which James had recommended. Tasso, who had enchanted her, 'But alas I yearn for what can never be!'

A woman coming out of a doorway eyed her suspiciously and Giulia wondered whether she had spoken the words aloud. 'Oh, never mind', she muttered as the woman went on. 'That's an old story anyway.'

She turned into a narrow street. Long shadows cut wedges off pavements and walls, ochre walls bristled with half-open vertical shutters. From some windows came voices, fragments of the latest song, the noise of plates being stacked up, echoing between the narrow walls. At the end of the street, she crossed the square towards Santa Maria del Carmine. She walked up the few steps which led to the unfinished façade and paused, caressing the rough stone facing. So many churches throughout the city had this uncared-for outside, so many of them were full of treasures within.

Someone came out and held the door open for her. Cool air invited her in. She walked down the nave towards the chancel, passing altar after altar, some with clusters of flickering candles. Faint noises reverberated. Incense lingered, its haze softened the lines of rising pillars, its acrid scent caught the throat and mingled with smoke from the smouldering wicks of expiring votive candles. The same smells as long ago. Sunday mornings at mass and the loving army of saints, and the smiling child Jesus made of painted plaster, and the first communion when good and evil were clearly laid out.

She crossed the transept to the Brancacci Chapel. Its walls were covered with frescoes, astonishingly fresh after so many centuries. She sat down and gazed at the figures, strong, made alive by the fresh colours.

Tourists came and went, alone or in groups.

She got up and walked to the box holding tall candles, chose one, put the coins into the wall slot and turned round to light it before putting it on the holder – only to realise there were none already lit and therefore no way of lighting her own.

'Signora. Would you like a match?'

She turned back towards the choir stalls. A black-robed figure sat there, observing her. He beckoned with his walking stick. As she went over to him, she suddenly recognised him, 'Fra Lodovico! How are you?'

'Getting older, as you can see. It's good to see you again, dear Giulia. How are you?'

'Well, thank you. Better than I was the last time I was here!'

'And how's the friend who was on your mind then?'

'We met, some months ago now. It's fine … But tell me, when did they finish the restoring of these beautiful frescoes? When I was here last, they were still hidden behind a green shroud. And now … they are stunning! So much more vivid than the first time I ever saw them.'

Fra Lodovico looked at her in silence for a few seconds, his eyes slightly squinting. Then he began to talk about the time it had taken to give back the frescoes the colours thought to be their original ones. Should she ask Fra Lodovico to pray for James? She could not bring herself to make such a request. She caught some words, 'time, research, painstaking labour of love' and realised she had not been listening.

In the evening, she had a salad in a trattoria she knew well, on the north side of the Duomo. Her mind drifted back to Fra Lodovico. How generous he had been with his time on her first visit to Florence. How easy she had found it to confide in him. A perfect stranger? Yes, but a monk, and her Catholic upbringing had trained her to view confession as natural, as was the assurance that whatever she said would stay undivulged. She had wondered, over the years, whether priests were still bound by the secret of the confessional when they were told – if they ever were – that someone had committed a murder or some other grave crime. But she had committed no murder, and her only crime had been to care too much for someone who did not …

Now she was, as far as she knew and fervently hoped, free from that bondage. She regretted having dismissed Fra Lodovico's question earlier. She felt she owed him – what? A kind of update? As a courtesy? A kindness to someone who had helped her? Her evasion this morning, her barely disguised refusal to answer his question, seemed mean to her now. She would go back to see him and be more open, more friendly. Give him an update. Tell him that James had died recently and ask him to pray for him? No. It would have seemed a betrayal to ask for prayers for someone who was such a convinced atheist. A help to her, possibly, but a betrayal of James all the same. However, she could tell Fra Lodovico that James was no more. He would understand her and would not insist on a requiem, spoken or otherwise.

LATHKILL DALE

Giulia walked past the Eurostar Terminal, the shops and cafés, and took the escalator to the East Midlands platforms. Her train was already there. She found her reserved seat and lodged her suitcase in the rack after taking her book from it.

They edged slowly out of the station, passing points and cabins, slowing down at some signal, moving past walls painted with adverts or dobbed with tags and graffiti. As they gathered speed, the façades of tightly-packed houses followed each other with increasing speed; then came sub-stations with illegible names; a stadium; a park with a few benches and tall trees. Embankments punctuated with a few touches of colour sped away, until the rhythm of the train settled and it began to glide smoothly past the fleeing shapes of houses and gardens.

She tried to draw a balance of the day she had spent with Rebecca, before her trip to Florence. It had been good to give her some time, to be able to help her with the rather untidy contents of the many folders in which James had kept his papers, mostly connected with his translations. Not so good to find the file containing her various suggestions about Ronsard starkly marked 'Brookes'. She hadn't expected it to be headed by James' favourite diminutive for her, but why hadn't he bothered with her first name? Why not even an initial? Just this impersonal, this remote, this cold, 'Brookes'. Was that the conclusion he had drawn from their association? Just a formal partnership, in spite of so many years teaching similar courses, discussing sonnets and translations? Just that, her surname and nothing else. It sent a stab right through to the pit of her stomach. It seemed to negate any of the warmth that had existed between them – or had it?

She settled in her seat and closed her eyes. James has died. James is no more. Any power he has, I'm giving him. In spite of herself, her mind went back to that folder, that impersonal surname, that indifferent heading. She wasn't mistaken, she had not misheard when he quoted poetry as if it had been written just for her. Not misheard, no, but perhaps misunderstood? She had been flattered, she had believed him – wanted to believe him?

The train jolted and stopped, forcing Giulia out of her musings. Her book slipped to the floor.[42] She picked it up, and thought, 'I am like Delmont: on a journey, looking for a change of heart. The only thing is, this is a book, up to the author to end it neatly. I may not be so lucky! All the same, it's a great book – and very appropriate for now. See what resolution of the remaining puzzle sharing it with Constance can bring!'

The first stop was Leicester, plenty of time for a nap, or for daydreaming. She kept her eyes closed. Time to switch over to Constance. The end of her journey would be Chesterfield and its crooked spire. Giulia and Constance

---

42 *La Modification* by Michel Butor, set in a train carriage on the journey Paris–Rome. The protagonist, Léon Delmont, reviews his relationship with his mistress Cécile who lives in Rome. The novel was published in 1957, hailed as a herald of the nouveau roman and translated several times into English under various titles: *Second Thoughts, A Change of Heart* and *Changing Track*.

often wondered how Chesterfield would attract tourists if the spire was not crooked; the town centre had little attraction for them. They much preferred Bakewell, with its many small shops and cafés. Bakewell, where health and safety regulations had stopped the poulterer hanging outside his shop braces of pheasants, or whatever local game was available. Nevertheless, Bakewell remained one of their favourite places to do a spot of food shopping when they spent a weekend together.

As for Chesterfield, it was a good meeting place. Constance would be waiting for her at the station, ready to whisk her away to a pub for their first drink of the evening before driving to 'The Cottage', as it was known – and revered – in the family. Constance had inherited this small, sturdy building on the main street of the village from a close and dear friend who had died young because of an undetected cancer. It lived up to its name of 'Dale View' because, from the lounge at the back and its bay window in which they took their meals, their eyes could embrace an uninterrupted view of the Dale sloping below, towards the river Lathkill. She and Constance often walked down to it, crossed the stream on a stone bridge, walked along the bank, crossed back over Conksbury and up the slope, talking as they walked.

She looked out of the window. It was getting dusk and she could just see the dark silhouettes of the trees, still bare of leaves, against the evening sky. A contrast with Florence, where spring was already on its way, and with the south of England, where it was ahead of here. Here, it was almost still winter, in spite of the snowdrops and crocuses piercing the green of the lawns in some of the parks. The trees were barely showing a green haze. She loved trees just before they gave in to spring. Trees still in the stark beauty of the clean lines of finishing winter. Poised as if they were waiting for a little more sun, a little more warmth to begin showing their leaves. For now, their outlines were still pure, unadorned delight. There wouldn't be too many trees on the hills around Dale View, but plenty along the river.

On Saturday morning, Constance made coffee and they sat, looking at the beautiful view, still and bathed in pale sunshine; a view as yet uninterrupted by the few trees on the hill sloping down to the Lathkill.

'Those trees … the spring has held back here. I am glad. I love to see the trees before they give in to the push of new leaves. Right now, they're sending me back to a day years ago,' said Giulia. 'Those trees ... you know how much I love their stark, pure beauty as they seem poised, almost holding still, as if on the brink of something. I was thinking of this on the train, as we passed some parks and some wooded areas.

It so reminds me of one particular time, with James, again. We were walking up Whitehall. It must have been this time of the year, because of the trees. But how long after we met? I can't be sure. Strange, because I usually have a good memory for dates. That day, he suddenly stopped – he was apt to do that – gently made me turn round so that he was standing behind me, both hands on my shoulders.

'I've told you he was much taller than I, so, when he spoke, he was slightly leaning down, his face touching my hair. Standing close behind me, he said softly, "Look, Giulietta, look. Right across the road: the Banqueting House. Inigo Jones." He loved that kind of building, Palladian, so gentle and beautifully balanced.'

Giulia paused and took a sip of her coffee. Constance sat very still, just listening. Giulia sighed. 'He said, "Beautiful. That building is just perfect as it is, and we can see it all. But see that tree in front of it? No leaves – and that's why the view is so pure. Another couple of weeks … another couple of weeks, Giulietta, and leaves will hide some of the beautiful façade." He was just whispering. Paused. Slightly tightened his hands on my shoulders, leant forward, so close to me. Then, he suddenly released the pressure on my shoulders, stood back and said, in a normal tone, "Beautiful things don't always last." He let go of me, turned away and resumed, on his own, his determined walk towards Trafalgar Square. Whilst I stood there, struggling to move, and trying to sense the meaning of it all.'

Constance had been to the kitchen to make a fresh pot of coffee. She filled up both cups and sat down again, saying, 'That's obviously a special memory. Did anything specific come from that day? Something which is why it still means so much to you? Still tugs at your heart?'

Giulia took another sip and sighed. 'Not really, that's the puzzling thing. He was a consummate artist at isolating one moment and making it special. Then, fool that I am, I took it as … oh, I don't quite know … but a kind of promise, a kind of progress – no, that's the wrong word.

Maybe an increase of trust between us, between what we felt free to tell the other in confidence? I thought it meant that we were getting more at ease with each other. But nine times out of ten, what I took as a proof of friendship just came to …. nothing.'

Constance smiled. 'It's a pattern you've often mentioned. Perhaps it's these sudden glimpses into a time when he could be gentle that make you reluctant to let go? I don't mean let go of the memories, they are as they are. I should know; you can't willingly erase them. But what I mean, perhaps, is … do you think they can ever lose their bite?'

Giulia sighed again. 'You may well ask. It's a question I often ask myself. Why should these still *stick* so much in my memory? Because they are precious? But why, if they also hurt? I can see … not sure how to put it … that, gentle as that moment was, it also had a sharp edge. Not in his last sentence, for it can be true – and that is sad. No, not in the words he said, but in the manner the tone changed, the manner in which he turned away, as he often did physically or in speech, as soon as he had given a hint of tenderness. From almost kissing me to dismissing me. From drawing me close to pushing me away. It happened often, and it always left me confused. Every time feeling drawn towards him, and then moved aside, pushed away. It was like walking on quicksand. All the time. But enough gloom. Tell me about your new, young acquaintance.'

Constance smiled. 'Tom? He is Rachel's new acquaintance rather than mine, although he has been here. I don't know him that much, but Rachel speaks of him as a true friend and, I have to say, I took to him instantly when he came here, some three weeks ago. He seemed so open, someone to be trusted.' She paused. 'Interesting, isn't it? If you draw a time line, starting with him and Rachel and ending with me, you seem to be in the middle. Generations separate each of us from the others ... and yet, we seem to be linked by strong bonds of friendship!'

She paused, looking out of the window to the fields sloping down towards the Lathkill.

'And linked by this area too – these hills and dales which, as you know, are to me the most beautiful place in the world. Rachel's love for this village, this cottage. And the place where Tom grew up, not far from here, near Derby, about an hour by car he says. And now you, who have come to love it as well. Come to love it through coming here, through this cottage, learnt to read and love this landscape.'

She lifted her cup of coffee as if to take another sip, put it down, and let her eyes wander over the room, to the many books on the shelves. 'Do you know what I thought of when I first saw Tom? *Tom's Midnight Garden.*'[43]

Giulia smiled. 'One of the very first books you introduced me to. Mentioning it brings back pictures of your school, your library. Such a beautiful book. So, if Rachel's new friend is Tom, who is Hatty?'

'Well, I could be,' said Constance. 'I could be young Hatty become old Mrs Bartholomew, since I am much older than he. *Time no longer*, as the clock-face says. That becomes a more and more enticing thought as you get older.'

---

43 *Tom's Midnight Garden*, a novel by Philippa Pearce, first published in 1958, is based on a 'time warp'. Meant for young readers, it is one of those books that appeal to readers of any age – provided they have a young heart!

Giulia smiled. 'I'm tempted to say, well, time doesn't always matter does it? Except that, if generations separate us from those we love, we know we shall be in their company for a shorter time. But then, isn't the connection, its strength, its quality ... isn't that what matters above all else?' She thought for a minute. 'Yet it also makes it harder when it comes to parting. I remember my friend Gilberte, the last few times I went to see her, she would walk with me to the gate, hug me before I left, hug me so hard... and say, "Oh, when shall I see you again? I hope I see you again!"'

Constance thought. 'True. But then, you can't let that colour every moment you have with friends, whatever their age. After all, we don't ever know what's round the corner. Yes, someone older is likely to die before someone younger, by the natural law of things.' She paused and finished her cup. 'Of course, it doesn't always work like that, but there's no point in brooding over it, is there? Carpe diem, I say! We're lucky to have this time together. Come on, have a bit more coffee and then we'll go into Bakewell and get some shopping.'

As they were having a light lunch in one of the many cafés boasting of selling the authentic Bakewell pudding, Giulia went back to their earlier talk.

'You said this morning that Rachel especially liked Tom's ideas about life. What's he like in that area?'

'One of the things, one of the prime truths Tom has shared with Rachel is the idea of ... fluidity.'

'Fluidity?'

'The fact that we are energy, vibration. That we are not static.'

'He doesn't mean there's no fixed point, no constancy in us?'

'No. I'm still mulling it over. It's a bit complicated for me, but Rachel is very interested and has explained it to me as best as she could. It has to do with the fact that we're not ... stolid? Inert? We're made of atoms, which do not remain still. I may be wrong and of course both Tom and Rachel are so much younger than I! But from my great age, I see it like this: I recognise you as you, and me as me, but even this you and this me aren't completely static. We're alive, made of atoms, and come into contact with the outside world ... and other people. And react to them. Think of our lives as circles: mine intersects with yours in one section; with Rachel's in another; which in turn intersects with Tom's. If there is one space in which all these lives intersect, then any one of the four is influenced, affected by the others and, in turn, affects others. I was thinking of this earlier when speaking of how this area links us four.'

'I hadn't thought of this in such terms. But it makes some sense. Well, Tom, Rachel and you are connected by this area anyway. As am I. But surely geography isn't enough? There has to be something deeper, more spiritual.' Giulia paused. 'I know. It can sound a bit pretentious, and yet some affinities do exist between people, for reasons that sometimes remain unclear to us. Think of Montaigne: he didn't know anything about atoms and vibrations, but when asked why he and his friend La Boétie were so close, his reply was, *"parce que c'était lui, parce que c'était moi"*.[44] So, without the knowledge of quantum physics, he'd hit the nail on the head! The French also speak of *atomes crochus* – literally, atoms that hook together spontaneously – or more elegantly of *affinités électives*. These I firmly believe in, where our friendship is concerned.'

Constance smiled. 'I agree! And it's also true for Rachel and me, for Rachel and Tom. But what about James?'

'James – I'm coming to think – what if I took his momentary tokens of affection – genuine but momentary, genuine but possibly skin-deep, and that's what I failed to see – what if I took these momentary tokens of affection as a constant of his character, when they were just … fleeting? Not only that, but I have to face the truth: he liked the odd thrill; but he also liked a quiet life. So, if I showed any sign of taking things seriously, he retreated. Where I read genuine, deep affection …,' Giulia finished her glass of wine and sighed. 'Hard to face, but what I took for signs of genuine affection may well have been true, superficially, but not worth rocking the boat. Hence the stories of his wife looking at him as if to turn him to stone if she saw my writing on an envelope, in order to stop me getting too earnest, which he saw as a potential danger. I don't believe that was ever true, not from the way Rebecca greeted me when we met for the first time at a conference – which was nice in a way, reassuring, but sad also, because then I realised James had lied. Another illusion shattered, the great man wasn't so great after all! The whole thing, which took up so much of my thinking,

---

[44] "because it was he, because it was I".

which weighed so much on my spirits, the whole thing could have been just a bit of flirting? Rebecca told me that he was prone to flirting with the pretty young nurses in the couple of years he spent in a home. Or, to put it in a simpler way, I was genuine, and he wasn't?'

Later, as the fire in the grate was roaring, Constance got out a new record. 'It's beautiful, at least I think so. Purcell's "Music for a while", sung by a new, emerging counter-tenor.'

As the pure notes rose, Giulia and Constance listened, sitting very still. 'Music for a while shall all your cares beguile.' Giulia smiled. 'For a while, that's the whole point, isn't it? For a while. Temporary again. Don't confuse temporary and permanent.'

'I didn't know whether to listen to this with you,' said Constance. 'Thought it might sadden you, with its emphasis on the fleeting, the impermanent. And yet, I wanted to share it with you.'

'You were right; it's beautiful. And, as far as James is concerned, I am beginning to feel a certain amount of resentment – not a nice feeling to nurture, but it has its uses in making the heart less sore. Occasional resentment towards him, but chiefly towards myself. For being so credulous. For being so flattered. For all the pain, which was unnecessary and childish. I feel this may be the beginning of a resolution. About time!'

'About time!' Such was Giulia's thought again as she sat in the train and looked out of the window, watching the spire of Chesterfield Cathedral gliding out of sight. Constance had dropped her at the station before getting back to Bakewell for an appointment. They would see each other again. Giulia already planned when she might be back – perhaps with a lighter heart.

BIBLIOGRAPHY

Chichester Record Office

'Draft Memorandum of agreement between William Smith, farmer of Chichester, and the Visiting Committee …for vacant possession of land', HCGR 6/4/3.

'General Rules For The Government Of The Asylum' (Charles Knight, Printer, Chichester).

Minute Book 2, 'Report of The Visiting Committee for providing a separate Asylum for West Sussex County, West Sussex County Lunatic Asylum'.

Minute Book 2, 'Report of the Visiting Committee July 1894–March 1898', West Sussex County Lunatic Asylum'.

Plan, copy 14756 dated 8th December 1892, showing farm in possession of William Smith, scale 6" to one mile.

'Regulations Pursuant to the 275th Section of the Lunacy Act, 1890' (Charles Knight, Printer, Chichester).

W.S.C.A. Rules, Regulations, Annual Reports 1898-1899-1900:

'First Report of the Medical Superintendent West Sussex County Asylum, May 27th, 1898' (Charles Knight, Printer, Chichester).

'Second Report of the Medical Superintendent, May 26th 1899'

'Second Annual Report of West Sussex County Asylum 1899'.

Other sources

BNP Paribas, 'Well of History', https://histoire.bnpparibas/en/bnp-paribas-at-the-heart-of-the-second-world-war/

Chapman, K., Ellender, L., Jaines, R. and Warren, R. (2023) *Nature's Calendar: The British Year in 72 Seasons* (Granta Books, London, ISBN 978-1-7837895-9-7)

Chichester City Council (1967) *The City Of Chichester* (18th edition)

The Graylingwell Heritage Project (2015) 'Beneath The Water Tower', www.graylingwellheritage.co.uk

Pearce, Philippa (2023 [1958]) *Tom's Midnight Garden* (Oxford University Press, ISBN 978-0-1927887-5-7)

Serio, Dr David (2017) *33* (CreateSpace, ISBN 978-1-9777832-3-3)

Taylor, Barbara (2014) *The Last Asylum: A Memoir Of Madness In Our Time* (Hamish Hamilton, ISBN 978-0-2411450-9-8)

ACKNOWLEDGEMENTS

Katherine Slay, former librarian at the Chichester Record Office, thank you for being always ready to help me access indispensable sources while I searched into the history of Graylingwell Hospital.

Chris, my husband, thank you for always giving me the time and space to write.

Thank you also to the few family and friends who cast a glance at some first drafts and offered comments.

Alison Shakspeare, it is a joy and a privilege to work with you. Thank you for your continued expert and friendly advice in matters both stylistic and technical. Your help in turning this book into a reality has been invaluable.

www.ingramcontent.com/pod-product-compliance
Lightning Source LLC
Chambersburg PA
CBHW061235070526
44584CB00030B/4141